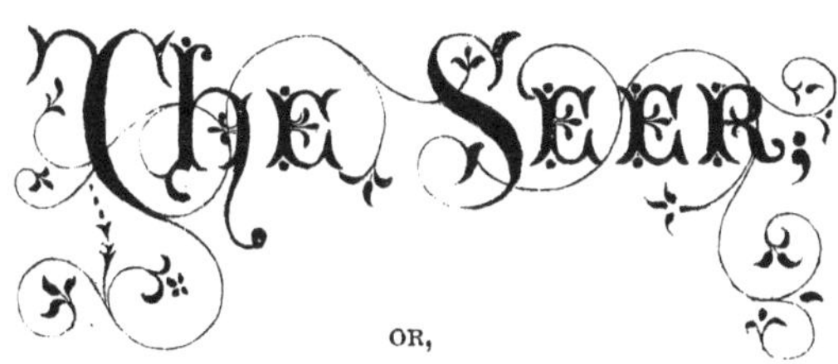

The Seer;

OR,

COMMON-PLACES REFRESHED.

By LEIGH HUNT.

IN TWO VOLUMES.

VOL. II.

LOVE ADDS A PRECIOUS SEEING TO THE EYE.—*Shakespeare.*

BOSTON:
ROBERTS BROTHERS, PUBLISHERS,
143, WASHINGTON STREET.
1864.

CONTENTS.

THE SEER;

OR,

COMMON-PLACES REFRESHED.

THE CAT BY THE FIRE.

BLAZING fire, a warm rug, candles lit and curtains drawn, the kettle on for tea (nor do the "first circles" despise the preference of a kettle to an urn, as the third or fourth may do), and finally, the cat before you, attracting your attention, — it is a scene which everybody likes, unless he has a morbid aversion to cats; which is not common. There are some nice inquirers, it is true, who are apt to make uneasy comparisons of cats with dogs, — to say they are not so loving, that they prefer the house to the man, &c. But agreeably to the good old maxim, that "comparisons are odious," our readers, we hope, will continue to like what is likable in any thing, for its own sake, without trying to render it unlikable from its inferiority to something else; a process by which we might ingeniously contrive to put soot into every dish that is set before us, and to reject one thing after another, till we were pleased with nothing. Here is a good fireside, and a cat to it; and it would be our own fault, if, in removing to another house and another fireside, we did not take care that the cat removed with us. Cats cannot look to the moving of goods, as men do. If we would have creatures considerate towards us, we must be so towards them. It is not to be expected of everybody, quadruped or biped, that they should stick to us in spite of our want of merit, like a dog or a benevolent sage. Besides, stories have been told of cats very much to the credit of their benignity; such as their following a master about like a dog, waiting at a gentleman's door to thank him for some obligation over night, &c. And our readers may remember the history of the famous Godolphin Arabian, upon whose grave a cat that had lived with him in the stable went and stretched itself, and died.

The cat purrs, as if it applauded our consideration; and gently moves its tail. What an odd expression of the power to be irritable and the will to be pleased there is in its face, as it looks up at us! We must own, that we do not prefer a cat in the act of purring, or of looking in that manner. It reminds us of the sort of smile or *simmer* (*simper* is too weak and fleeting a word) that is apt to be in the faces of irritable people when they are pleased to be in a state of satisfaction. We prefer, for a general expression, the cat in a quiet, unpretending state; and the human countenance with a look indicative of habitual grace and composure, as if it were not necessary to take any violent steps to prove its amiability,—the "smile without a smile," as the poet beautifully calls it.*

Furthermore (in order to get rid at once of all that may be objected to poor Pussy, as boys at school get down their bad dumpling as fast as possible, before the meat comes), we own we have an objection to the way in which a cat sports with a mouse before she kills it, tossing and jerking it about like a ball, and letting it go, in order to pounce upon it with the greater relish. And yet what right have we to apply human measures of cruelty to the inferior reflectibility of a cat? Perhaps she has no idea of the mouse's being alive, in the sense that we have: most likely she looks upon it as a pleasant movable toy, made to be eaten,—a sort of lively pudding, that oddly jumps hither and thither. It would be hard to beat into the head of a country squire, of the old class, that there is any cruelty in hunting a hare; and most assuredly it would be still harder to beat mouse-sparing into the head of a cat. You might read the most pungent essay on the subject into her ear, and she would only sneeze at it.

As to the unnatural cruelties, which we sometimes read of, committed by cats upon their offspring, they are exceptions to the common and beautiful rules of nature; and, accordingly, we have nothing to do with them. They are traceable to some unnatural circumstances of breeding or position. Enormities as monstrous are to be found among human beings, and argue nothing against the general character of the

* Knowles, in the "Beggar of Bethnal Green."

species. Even dogs are not always immaculate; and sages have made slips. Dr. Franklin cut off his son with a shilling, for differing with him in politics.

But cats resemble tigers? They are tigers in miniature? Well, — and very pretty miniatures they are. And what has the tiger himself done, that he has not a right to his dinner, as well as Jones? A tiger treats a man much as a cat does a mouse: — granted; but we have no reason to suppose that he is aware of the man's sufferings, or means any thing but to satisfy his hunger; and what have the butcher and poulterer been about, meanwhile? The tiger, it is true, lays about him a little superfluously sometimes, when he gets into a sheepfold, and kills more than he eats; but does not the squire or the marquis do pretty much like him in the month of September? Nay, do we not hear of venerable judges, that would not hurt a fly, going about in that refreshing month, seeking whom they may lame? See the effect of habit and education! And you can educate the tiger in no other way than by attending to his stomach. Fill that, and he will want no men to eat, probably not even to lame. On the other hand, deprive Jones of his dinner for a day or two, and see what a state he will be in, especially if he is by nature irascible. Nay, keep him from it for an half an hour, and observe the tiger propensities of his stomach and fingers, — how worthy of killing he thinks the cook, and what boxes of the ear he feels inclined to give the footboy.

Animals, by the nature of things, in their present state, dispose of one another into their respective stomachs, without ill-will on any side. They keep down the several populations of their neighbors, till time may come when superfluous population of any kind need not exist, and predatory appearances may vanish from the earth, as the wolves have done from England. But whether they may or not, is not a question by a hundred times so important to moral inquirers, as into the possibilities of human education and the nonsense of ill-will. Show the nonentity of that, and we may all get our dinners as jovially as we can; sure of these three undoubted facts, — that life is long, death short, and the world beautiful. And so we bring our thoughts back again to the fireside, and look at the cat.

Poor Pussy! she looks up at us again, as if she thanked us for those vindications of dinner; and symbolically gives a twist of a yawn, and a lick to her whiskers. Now she proceeds to clean herself all over, having a just sense of the demands of her elegant person, — beginning judiciously with her paws, and fetching amazing tongues at her hind-hips. Anon, she scratches her neck with a foot of rapid delight; leaning her head towards it, and shutting her eyes, half to accommodate the action of the skin, and half to enjoy the luxury. She then rewards her paws with a few more touches. Look at the action of her head and neck, how pleasing it is, the ears pointed forward, and the neck gently arching to and fro! Finally, she gives a sneeze, and another twist of mouth and whiskers, and then, curling her tail towards her front claws, settles herself on her hind-quarters, in an attitude of bland meditation.

What does she think of? Of her saucer of milk at breakfast? or of the thump she got yesterday in the kitchen for stealing the meat? or of her own meat, the Tartar's dish, noble horse-flesh? or of her friend the cat next door, the most impassioned of serenaders? or of her little ones, some of whom are now large, and all of them gone? Is *that* among her recollections when she looks pensive? Does she taste of the noble prerogative-sorrows of man?

She is a sprightly cat, hardly past her youth: so, happening to move the fringe of the rug a little with our foot, she darts out a paw, and begins plucking it and inquiring into the matter, as if it were a challenge to play, or something lively enough to be eaten. What a graceful action of that foot of hers, between delicacy and petulance! — combining something of a thrust-out, a beat, and a scratch. There seems even something of a little bit of fear in it, as if just enough to provoke her courage, and give her the excitement of a sense of hazard. We remember being much amused with seeing a kitten manifestly making a series of experiments upon the patience of its mother, — trying how far the latter would put up with positive bites and thumps. The kitten ran at her every moment, gave her a knock or a bite of the tail, and then ran back again, to recommence the assault. The mother sat looking at her, as if betwixt tolerance and admiration, to see how far the spirit of the family was inherited or improved by her sprightly offspring. At length, however, the "little Pickle" presumed too far; and the mother, lifting up her paw, and meeting her at the very nick of the moment, gave her one of the most unsophisticated boxes of the ear we ever beheld. It sent her rolling half over the room, and made her come to a most ludicrous pause, with the oddest little look of premature and wincing meditation.

That lapping of the milk out of the saucer is what one's human thirst cannot sympathize with. It seems as if there could be no satisfaction in such a series of atoms of drink. Yet the saucer is soon emptied; and there is a refreshment to one's ears in that sound of plashing with which the action is accompanied, and which seems indicative of a like comfort to Pussy's mouth. Her tongue is thin, and can make a spoon of itself. This, however, is common to other quadrupeds with the cat, and does not, therefore, more particularly belong to our feline consideration. Not so the electricity of its coat, which gives out sparks under the hand; its passion for the herb valerian (did the reader ever see one roll in it? it is a mad sight) and other singular delicacies of nature, among which perhaps is to be reckoned its taste for fish, a creature with whose element it has so little to do, that it is supposed even to abhor it; though lately we read somewhere of a swimming cat, that used to fish for itself. And this reminds us of an exquisite anecdote of dear, dogmatic, diseased, thoughtful, surly, charitable Johnson, who would go out of doors himself, and buy oysters for his cat, because his black servant was too proud to do it! Not that we condemn the black, in those enslaving, unliberating days. He had a right to the mistake, though we should have thought better of him had he seen farther, and subjected his pride to affection for such a master. But Johnson's true practical delicacy in the matter is beautiful. Be assured that he thought nothing of "condescension" in it, or of being eccentric. He was singular in some things, because he could not help it. But he hated eccentricity. No: in his best moments, he felt himself simply to be a man, and a good man too, though a frail, — one that in virtue as well as humility, and in a knowledge of his ignorance as well as his wisdom, was desirous of being a Christian philosopher; and, accordingly, he went out and bought food for his hungry cat, because his poor negro was too proud to do it, and there was nobody else in the way whom he had a right to ask. What must anybody that saw him have thought, as he turned up Bolt Court! But doubtless he went as secretly as possible; that is to say, if he considered the thing at all. His friend Garrick could not have done as much! He was too grand, and on the great "stage" of life. Goldsmith could; but he would hardly have thought of it. Beauclerc might; but he would have thought it necessary to excuse it with a jest or a wager, or some such thing. Sir Joshua Reynolds, with his fashionable, fine-lady-painting hand, would certainly have shrunk from it. Burke would have reasoned himself into its propriety, but he would have reasoned himself out again. Gibbon! — imagine its being put into the head of Gibbon! He and his bag-wig would have started with all the horror of a gentleman-usher; and he would have rung the bell for the cook's-deputy's-under-assistant-errand-boy.

Cats at firesides live luxuriously, and are the picture of comfort; but, lest they should not bear their portion of trouble in this world, they have the drawbacks of being liable to be shut out of doors on cold nights, beatings from the "aggravated" cooks, over-pettings of children, (how should we like to be squeezed and pulled about in that manner by some great patronizing giants?) and last, not least, horrible merciless tramples of unconscious human feet and unfeeling legs of chairs. Elegance, comfort, and security seem the order of the day on all sides; and you are going to sit down to dinner, or to music, or to take tea, when all of a sudden the cat gives a squall, as if she was mashed; and you are not sure that the fact is otherwise. Yet she gets in the way again, as before; and dares all the feet and mahogany in the room. Beautiful present sufficingness of a cat's imagination!—confined to the snug circle of her own sides, and the two next inches of rug or carpet.

PUT UP A PICTURE IN YOUR ROOM.

MAY we exhort such of our readers as have no pictures hanging in their room to put one up immediately?—we mean in their principal sitting-room: in all their rooms, if possible; but, at all events, in that one. No matter how costly, or the reverse, provided they *see something in it*, and it gives them a profitable or pleasant thought. Some may allege that they have "no taste for pictures;" but they have a taste for objects to be found in pictures,—for trees, for landscapes, for human beauty, for scenes of life; or, if not for all these, yet surely for some one of them: and it is highly useful for the human mind to give itself helps towards taking an interest in things apart from its immediate cares or desires. They serve to refresh us for their better conquest or endurance; to render sorrow unselfish; to remind us that we ourselves, or our own personal wishes, are not the only objects in the world; to instruct and elevate us, and put us in a fairer way of realizing the good opinions which we would all fain entertain of ourselves, and in some measure do; to make us compare notes with other individuals, and with Nature at large, and correct our infirmities at their mirror by modesty and reflection; in short, even the admiration of a picture is a kind of religion, or additional tie on our consciences, and *rebinding* of us (for such is the meaning of the word "religion") to the greatness and goodness of Nature.

Mr. Hazlitt has said somewhere, of the portrait of a beautiful female with a noble countenance, that it seems as if an unhandsome action would be impossible in its presence. It is not so much for restraint's sake, as for the sake of diffusiveness of heart or the going-out of ourselves, that we would recommend pictures; but, among other advantages, this also, of reminding us of our duties, would doubtless be one; and, if reminded with charity, the effect, though perhaps small in most instances, would still be something. We have read of a Catholic money-lender, who, when he was going to cheat a customer, always drew a veil over the portrait of his favorite saint. Here was a favorite vice, far more influential than the favorite saint; and yet we are of opinion that the money-lender was better for the saint than he would have been without him. It left him faith in something; he was better for it in the intervals; he would have treated his daughter the better for it, or his servant, or his dog. There was a bit of heaven in his room, — a sunbeam to shine into a corner of his heart, — however he may have shut the window against it when heaven was not to look on.

The companionship of any thing greater or better than ourselves must do us good, unless we are destitute of all modesty or patience; and a picture is a companion, and the next thing to the presence of what it represents. We may live in the thick of a city, for instance, and can seldom go out and "feed" ourselves —

"With pleasure of the breathing fields;"

but we can put up a picture of the fields before us, and, as we get used to it, we shall find it the next thing to seeing the fields at a distance. For every picture is a kind of window, which supplies us with a fine sight; and many a thick, unpierced wall thus lets us into the studies of the greatest men and the most beautiful scenes of nature. By living with pictures, we learn to "read" them, — to see into every nook and corner of a landscape, and every feature of the mind; and it is impossible to be in the habit of these perusals, or even of being vaguely conscious of the presence of the good and beautiful, and considering them as belonging to us, or forming a part of our commonplaces, without being, at the very least, less subject to the disadvantages arising from having no such thoughts at all.

And it is so easy to square the picture to one's aspirations or professions, or the powers of one's pocket. For, as to resolving to have no picture at all in one's room, unless we could have it costly, and finely painted, and finely framed, that would be a mistake so vulgar, that we trust no reader of any decent publication now-a-days could fall into it. The greatest knave or simpleton in England, provided he is rich, can procure one of the finest paintings in the world to-morrow, and know nothing about it when he has got it: but to feel the beauties of a work of art, or to be capable of being led to feel them, is a gift which often falls to the lot of the poorest; and this is what

Raphael or Titian desired in those who looked at their pictures. All the rest is taking the clothes for the man. Now, it so happens that the cheapest engravings, though they cannot come up to the merits of the originals, often contain no mean portion or shadow of them: and, when we speak of putting pictures up in a room, we use the word "picture" in the child's sense; meaning any kind of graphic representation, — oil, water-color, copperplate, drawing, or woodcut; and any one of these is worth putting up in your room, provided you have mind enough to get a pleasure from it. Even a frame is not necessary, if you cannot afford it. Better put up a rough, varnished engraving, than none at all, — or pin, or stick up, any engraving whatsoever, at the hazard of its growing never so dirty. You will keep it as clean as you can, and for as long a time; and as for the rest, it is better to have a good memorandum before you, and get a fresh one when you are able, than to have none at all, or even to keep it clean in a portfolio. How should you like to keep your own heart in a portfolio, or lock your friend up in another room? We are no friends to portfolios, except where they contain more prints than can be hung up. The more, in that case, the better.

Our readers have seen in all parts of the country, over the doors of public-houses, "Perkins and Co.'s Entire." This Perkins, who died wealthy a few years ago, was not a mere brewer or rich man. He had been head-clerk to Thrale, the friend of Dr. Johnson; and, during his clerkship, the doctor, happening to go into his counting-house, saw a portrait of himself (Johnson) hanging up in it. "How is this, sir?" inquired Johnson. "Sir," said Perkins, "I was resolved that my room should have one great man in it."—"A very pretty compliment," returned the gratified moralist; "and I believe you mean it sincerely."

Mr. Perkins did not thrive the worse for having the portrait of Johnson in his counting-house. People are, in general, quite enough inclined to look after the interests of "number one:" but they make a poor business of it, rich as they may become, unless they include a power of forgetting it in behalf of number two; that is to say, of some one person or thing, besides themselves, able to divert them from mere self-seeking. It is not uncommon to see one solitary portrait in a lawyer's office, and that portrait a lawyer's; generally some judge. It is better than none. Any thing is better than the poor, small unit of a man's selfish self, even if it be but the next thing to it. And there is the cost of the engraving and frame. Sometimes there is more: for these professional prints, especially when alone, are meant to imply that the possessor is a shrewd, industrious, proper lawyer, who sticks to his calling, and wastes his time in "no nonsense;" and this ostentation of business is, in some instances, a cover for idleness or disgust, or a blind for a father or rich uncle. Now, it would be better, we think, to have two pictures instead of one, — the judge's, by all means, for the professional part of the gentleman's soul; and some one other picture to show his client that he is a man as well as a lawyer, and has an eye to the world outside of him as well as to his own: for as men come from that world to consult him, and generally think their cases just in the eyes of common sense as well as law, they like to see that he has some sympathies as well as cunning.

Upon these grounds, it would be well for men of other callings if they acted in a similar way. The young merchant should reasonably have a portrait of some eminent merchant before his eyes, with some other, not far off, to hinder him from acknowledging no merit but in riches. Or he might select a merchant of such a character as could serve both uses, — Sir Thomas Gresham, for instance, who encouraged knowledge as well as money-getting; or Lorenzo de Medici, the princely merchant of Italy. So with regard to clergymen, to professions of all sorts, and to trade. The hosier, in honor of his calling, might set up Defoe, who was one of that trade, as well as author of "Robinson Crusoe;" the bookseller may the footman Dodsley, who was at one time a footman as well as a bookseller and author, and behaved excellently under all characters; and the tailor might balk petty animadversions on his trade, by having a portrait, or one of the many admirable works, of the great Annibal Caracci, who was a tailor's son. It would be advisable, in general, to add a landscape, if possible, for reasons already intimated; but a picture of some sort we hold to be almost indispensably necessary towards doing justice to the habitation of every one who is capable of reflection and improvement. The print-shops, the bookstalls, the portfolios containing etchings and engravings at a penny or twopence apiece (often superior to plates charged twenty times as much), and, lastly, the engravings that make their way into the shop-windows, out of the annuals of the past season, and that are to be had for almost as little, will furnish the ingenuous reader of this article with an infinite store to choose from; and, if he is as good-natured as he is sensible, we will venture to whisper into his ear, that we should take it as a personal kindness of him, and hope he would consider us as a friend assisting him in putting it up.

A GENTLEMAN-SAINT.

Beauties of St. Francis de Sales.

LOOKING over the catalogue, the other day, of Mr. Cawthorn's excellent circulating library (which has the books it professes to have, — a rare virtue in such establishments), our curiosity was raised by a volume entitled "Beauties of St. Francis de Sales." We sent for it, and found we had started so delicious a saint, that we vowed we must make him known to our readers. He is a true godsend, a man of men, a real quintessence of Christian charity, and shrewd sense withal (things not only far from incompatible, but thoroughly amalgamable); in short, a man as sensible as Dr. Johnson, with all the piety and patience which the doctor desired to have, all the lowliness and kind fellowship which it would have puzzled him to behold in a prelate, and all the delicacy and true breeding which would have transported him. Like Fénélon, he was a sort of angel of a gentleman, a species of phœnix, which, we really must say, the French Church seems to have produced beyond any other. Not that we undervalue the Hookers and Jewels, and other primitive excellences of our own: deeply do we love and venerate them. But we like to see a human being develop all the humanities of which he is capable, — those of outward as well as inward elegance not excepted; not indeed in the inconsistent and foppish shape of a Sir Charles Grandison (who comes hushing upon us with insinuations of equal perfection in dancing and the decalogue, with soft deprecations of our astonishment, and all sorts of equivocal worldly accomplishments, which the author has furnished him with, on purpose to keep his piety safe, — swordsmanship, for one), but in whatsoever, being the true spirit of a gentleman, manifests itself outwardly in consequence, — shaping the movements of the commonest and most superficial parts of life to the unaffected elegance of the spirit within; and, at the same time, refusing no fellowship with honesty of any sort, nor ostentatiously claiming it; but feeling and having it, because of its true, natural, honest heart's blood, and a tendency to relish all things in common with us, "passioned as we."

When a man exhibits this nature, as St. Francis de Sales did, and exhibits it, too, in the shape of a mortified saint of the Romish Church, a lone lodger, a celibatory, entering into everybody else's wishes and feelings, but denying himself some of the most precious to a being so constituted, we feel proud for the sake of the capabilities of humanity; proud because we belong to a species which we are utterly unable to illustrate so in our own persons; proud and happy and hopeful, that, if one human being can do so much, thousands, nay all, by like opportunities, and a like loving breeding, may ultimately do; not indeed the same, but enough, — enough for themselves, and enough for the like exalted natures, too, who have the luck to live in such times.

Even if such times are not to come, but are merely among the fancies or necessary activities of the human mind, then still we are grateful for the vision by the way, and, above all, for the exquisite real fellowship.

We need not deprecate any ill construction of our use of the term "gentleman-saint." In some sort, we do confess, we use it with a delighted smile on our face, astonished to start such a phenomenon in high life; but, while the conversational sense of the word is included, we claim for it, as we have explained, the very largest and truest sense. One of our brave old English dramatists — brave because his humanity misgave him in nothing — dared to call the divinest of beings that have trod the earth —

> "The first true gentleman that ever breathed."

Here is another (at far distance) of the same heraldry, his shield —

> "Heart-shaped, and vermeil-dyed."

Fénélon was another, but not so active or persuasive as De Sales. St. Vincent de Paul, if we mistake not, the founder of the Sisters of Charity, was a fourth. So, we believe, was St. Thomas Aquinas. So, perhaps, was Jeremy Taylor, and certainly Berkeley, — the latter the more unquestionably of the two, because he was the more active in doing good, and manifestly did not care twopence for honors and profits, compared with the chance of benefiting his fellow-creatures. At one time, for this purpose, he *petitioned* to give up his preferments! Swift has a pleasant passage in furtherance of this object, in which he tells the Lord-Lieutenant of Ireland, that Dr. Berkeley will be miserable in case he is not allowed to give up some hundreds a year.

We will first give the "General Biographical Dictionary" account of St. Francis de Sales, and follow it with a notice of the book before us:—

"St. Francis de Sales was born at the Castle of Sales, in the diocese of Geneva, Aug. 21, 1567. He descended from one of the most ancient and noble families of Savoy. Having taken a doctor of law's degree at Padua, he was first advocate at Chambery, then provost of the church of Geneva at Annecy. Claudius de Granier, his bishop, sent him as a missionary into the valleys of his diocese to convert the Zuinglians and Calvinists, which he is said to have performed in great numbers (*sic*), and his sermons were attended with wonderful success. The bishop of Geneva chose him afterwards for his coadjutor, but was obliged to use authority before he could be persuaded to accept the office. Religious affairs called him afterwards into France, where he was universally esteemed; and Cardinal du Perron said, 'There were no heretics whom he could not convince, but M. de Geneva must be employed to convert them.' Henry IV., being informed of his merit, made him considerable offers, in hopes of detaining him in France; but he chose rather to return to Savoy, where he arrived in 1602, and found Bishop Granier had died a few days before. St. Francis then undertook the reformation of his diocese, where piety and virtue soon flourished through his zeal: he restored regularity in the monasteries, and instituted the order of the Visitation in 1610, which was confirmed by Paul V., 1618, and of which the Baroness de Chantal, whom he converted by his preaching at Dijon, was the foundress. He also established a congregation of hermits in Chablais, restored ecclesiastical discipline to its ancient vigor, and converted numerous heretics to the faith. At the latter end of 1618, St. Francis was obliged to go again to Paris, with the Cardinal de Savoy, to conclude a marriage between the Prince of Piedmont and Christina of France, second daughter of Henry IV. This princess herself chose De Sales for her chief almoner; but he would accept the place only on two conditions: one, that it should not preclude his residing in his diocese; the other, that, whenever he did not execute his office, he should not receive the profits of it. These unusual terms the princess was obliged to consent to; and immediately, as if by way of investing him with his office, presented him with a very valuable diamond, saying, 'On condition that you will keep it for my sake.' To which he replied, 'I promise to do so, madam, unless the poor stand in need of it.' Returning to Annecy, he continued to visit the sick, relieve those in want, instruct the people, and discharge all the duties of a pious bishop, till 1662; when he died of an apoplexy at Lyons, Dec. 28, aged fifty-six, leaving several religious works, collected in two vols. folio. The most known are the 'Introduction to a Devout Life;' and 'Philo, or a Treatise on the Love of God.' Marsollier has written his life (two vols. 12mo), which was translated into English by Mr. Crathorne. He was canonized in 1665." — MORERI: *Dict. Hist.* — Butler.

The writers of this notice do not seem to have been aware, that Camus, Bishop of Bellay, the disciple and friend of St. Francis, wrote a large account of him, "the Beauties" of which the work before us professes to give the public. This English volume is itself a curiosity. It is printed at Barnet, and emanates most likely from some public-spirited enthusiast of the Roman-Catholic persuasion, who has thought — not without reason — to sow a good seed in these strange, opinion-conflicting, yet truth-desiring times, when a little *genuine* Christianity stands a chance of being well received, from whatever quarter it comes. A friend of ours, smitten with love of the book, has applied for a copy at Messrs. Longman's, whose name is in the titlepage, but is told that they have not one left: so that, if the Barnet press do not take Christian pity upon the curious, we know not what is to be done for them, apart from the following extracts; which, however, we take to be quite enough to set any handsome mind upon salutary reflections.

Camus, the Boswell of a saint, is himself a curiosity. He was a man of wit and a satirist, and so far (in the latter respect) not very well fitted for ultra Christian aspiration. But he was also an enthusiastic lover of goodness, and of his great seraphical friend; whom he looked up to with all the congregated humilities of a younger age, a real self-knowledge, and an unaffected modesty. He was naturally as hasty in his temperament as St. Francis was the reverse; and was always for getting on too fast, and being angry that others would not be Christian enough: and it is quite delightful to see with what sense and good-humor his teacher reproves him, and sets him in the right way; upon which the young bishop begins over-emulating the older one (for they were both prelates together), trying to imitate his staid manners and deliberate style of preaching; and then St. Francis reproves him again, joking as well as reasoning, and showing how he was spoiling the style peculiar to himself (Camus), with no possibility of getting at the style of another man, — the result of his habits and particular turn of mind.

But let the reader see for himself what a nature this man had, — what wisdom with simplicity, what undeviating kindness, what shrewd worldly discernment with unworldly feelings; what capital Johnsonian good sense, and wit too, and illustration, sometimes as familiar as any table-talk could desire, at others in the very depth of the heart of sentiment and poetical grace. Observe also what a proper saint he was for every day, as well as for holidays; and how he could sit down at table, and be an ordinary, unaffected gentleman among gentlemen, and dine at less elegant tables at inns, and say a true honest word, with not a syllable of pretence in it, for your hard-working innkeeper, — "publican," and perhaps "sinner," as he was.

"Beautiful are the ceremonies of the church!" said a Roman-Catholic prelate, when a great wax-candle was brought before him, stuck full of pieces of gold (his perquisite). "Beautiful are the ceremonies of the church!" think we, also, though no Roman Catholic, when we hear the organ roll, and the choir-voices rising, and see the white wax-candles on the altar, and the dark glowing paintings, full of hopeful or sweet-suffering faces. But most truly beautiful, certainly, must they have been, when they had such a man as this St. Francis de Sales ministering at the altar, and making those seraphical visions true in the shape of an every-day human being. But to our extracts: —

" In speaking of brotherly correction (says the good Bishop Camus), St. Francis gave me a lesson which I have not forgotten. He repeated it often, the better to impress it on my memory. '*That sincerity*,' said he, '*which is not charitable, proceeds from a charity which is not sincere.*' A worthy saying, worthy of being deeply considered and faithfully remembered.

" IT IS BETTER TO REMAIN SILENT THAN SPEAK THE TRUTH ILL-HUMOREDLY, AND SO SPOIL AN EXCELLENT DISH BY COVERING IT WITH BAD SAUCE.

" I asked St. Francis if there were no other way by which I might discern from what fountain reproaches flowed. He, whose heart was wrapped up in benevolence, replied, in the true spirit of the great apostle, 'When they are made with mildness, *Mildness is the sister of Love, and inseparable from her*. With this idea, St. Paul says, " she beareth all things, believeth all things, hopeth all things, endureth all things." God, *who is charity*, guides the meek with his counsel, and teaches his ways to the simple. His spirit is not in the hurricane, the foaming cataract, or the tempestuous winds, but in the soft breath of the gentle zephyr. " Is mildness come ? " said the prophet : " then are we corrected." I advise you to imitate the Good Samaritan, who poured oil and wine into the wounds of the unhappy traveller. *You know, that, in a good salad, there should be more oil than vinegar or salt.* Be always as mild as you can: a spoonful of honey attracts more flies than a barrel of vinegar. *If you must fall into any extreme, let it be on the side of gentleness.* The human mind is so constructed, that it resists rigor, and yields to softness. A mild word quenches anger, as water quenches the rage of fire; and, by benignity, any soil may be rendered fruitful. Truth, uttered with courtesy, is heaping coals of fire on the head; or, *rather*, THROWING ROSES IN THE FACE. *How can we resist a foe whose weapons are pearls and diamonds?* Some fruits, like nuts, are by nature bitter, but rendered sweet by being candied with sugar: such is reproof, bitter till candied with meekness, and preserved with the fire of charity.'

"St. Francis always *discouraged professions of humility*, if they were not *very* true and *very* sincere. 'Such professions,' he said, 'are the very cream, the very essence, of pride: the real humble man wishes to be, and not to appear so. Humility is timorous, and starts at her shadow; and so delicate, that, *if she hears her name pronounced, it endangers her existence.* He who blames himself takes a by-road to praise; and, like the rower, turns his back to the place whither he desires to go. *He would be irritated if what he said against himself were believed;* but, from a principle of pride, he desires to appear humble.'

"I esteemed my friend (resumes excellent Camus) so highly, that all his actions appeared to me perfect. It came into my head that it would be a very good thing to copy his manner of preaching. Do not suppose that I attempted to equal him in the loftiness of his ideas, in the depth of his arguments, in the strength of his reasonings, in the excellence of his judgment, the mildness of his expressions, the order and just connection of his periods, or that incomparable sweetness which could soften the hardest heart: no; that was quite beyond my powers. I was like a fly, which, not being able to walk on the polished surface of a mirror, is contented to remain on the frame which surrounds it. I amused myself in copying his gesture, in conforming myself to his slow and quiet manner of pronouncing and moving. My own manner was naturally the very reverse of all this: the metamorphosis was therefore so strange, that I was scarcely to be recognized. I was no longer myself. I contrived to spoil my own original manner, without acquiring the admirable one which I so idly copied.

" St. Francis heard of this, and one day took an opportunity of saying to me, 'Speaking of sermons reminds me of a strange piece of news which has reached my ears. It is reported that you try, in preaching, to adopt the Bishop of Geneva's peculiarities.' I warded off this reproof by saying, 'And do you think I have chosen a bad example? What is your opinion of the Bishop of Geneva's preaching?'—'*Ha!*' said he, '*this grave question attacks reputation. Why, he really does not preach badly;* but the fact is, that you are accused of being *so bad a mimic*, that nothing is to be seen but an unsuccessful attempt, which *spoils the Bishop of Bellay, without representing the Bishop of Geneva.* So that you ought to do as a bad painter did: he wrote under his pictures the name of the objects which they misrepresented.'—'Let them talk,' said I, 'and you will find, that, by degrees, the apprentice will become master, and the copies be mistaken for originals.'—'Joking apart,' rejoined my friend, 'you do yourself an injury. Why demolish a well-built edifice to erect one in its stead in which no rules of nature or art are adhered to? and at your age, if you once take a wrong bias, it will be difficult to set you right again. *If natures could be exchanged*, gladly would I exchange *with you. I do all I can to rouse myself to animation. I try to be less tedious; but*, *the more haste I make*, *the more I impede my course.* I have difficulty in finding words, and greater still in pronouncing them. I am as slow as a tortoise. I can neither raise emotion in myself nor in my auditors. All my labor to do so is inefficient. You advance with crowded sail: I make my way with rowing. You fly: I creep. You have more fire in one finger than I have in my whole body. Your readiness and promptitude are wonderful, your vivacity unequalled; and now people say you weigh each word, count every period, appear languid yourself, and weary your audience.' *You may well imagine how this well-timed reproof and commendation cured my folly. I returned immediately to my original manner.*

"'The best fish are nourished in the *unpalatable waters* of the sea, and the best souls are improved by *such opposition as does not extinguish charity*.'

"I asked St. Francis what disposition of mind was the best with which to meet death. He coolly replied, '*A charitable disposition.*'

"Do not overrate the blessings which God gives to others, and then underrate or despise what are given to yourself. It is the property of a little mind to say, 'Our neighbor's harvest is always more plentiful than our own, and his flock more prosperous.'

"I complained of some great hardships which I had experienced: it was obvious that St. Francis agreed in thinking that I had been ill treated. Finding myself so well seconded, *I was triumphant*, and *exaggerated* the justice of my cause in a superfluity of words. To stop the torrent of complaint, St. Francis said, 'Certainly they are wrong in treating you in this manner. It is beneath them to do so, especially to a man in your condition; but, in the whole of the business, I see only one thing to your disadvantage.'—'What is that?'—'*That you might have been wiser, and remained silent!*' This answer came so immediately home to me, that I felt immediately silenced, and found it impossible to make any reply."

The following was a strange bit of supererogation in the lively Bishop of Bellay. His candor hardly excuses it; yet it increases our interest in his friend.

"St. Francis practised himself the lessons which he taught to others; and during fourteen years that I was under his direction, and made it my study to remark all his actions, and even his very gestures and words, I never observed in him the slightest affectation of singularity. I will confess one of my contrivances when he visited me in my own house, and remained, as his custom was, a week annually: *I contrived to bore holes, by which I saw him when alone*, engaged in study, prayer, or reading, meditating, dressing, sitting, walking, or writing, when usually persons are most off their guard; yet I could not trace any difference in attitude or manner: his behavior was ever as sincere and undisguised as his heart. He had, when alone, the same dignified manners as when in society: *when he prayed, you would have imagined that he saw himself surrounded by holy angels;* motionless, and with a countenance of humble reverence. I never saw him indulge in any indolent attitude (!), neither crossing his legs, nor resting his head on his hand: at all times he presented the same aspect of mingled gravity and sweetness, which never failed to inspire love and respect. He used to say that *our manners should resemble water,—best when clearest, most simple, and without taste.* However, though he had no peculiarities of behavior, it appeared so singular that he should have no singularities, that he struck me, therefore, as very singular.

"WILLINGLY, NOT BY CONSTRAINT.

"This was my friend's favorite saying, and the secret of his government. He used to say that those who would force the human will exercise a tyranny odious to God. He never could bear those haughty persons who would be obeyed, whether willingly or not, they cared not. 'Those,' he said, 'who love to be feared, fear to be loved: they themselves are of all people the most abject: some fear them, but they fear every one. *In the royal galley of Divine Love there is no force: the rowers are all volunteers.*' On this principle he always moulded his commands into the softer form of entreaty. St. Peter's words, 'Feed the flock of God, not by constraint,' he was very fond of. I complained of the resistance I met with in my parochial visits. 'What a commanding spirit you have!' he replied: 'you want to walk on the wings of the wind, and you let yourself be carried away with zeal. Like an *ignis-fatuus*, it leads to the edge of precipices. *Do you seek to shackle the will of man, when God has seen fit to have it free?'*

"St. Francis did not approve of the saying, — 'Never rely on a reconciled enemy.' He rather preferred a contrary maxim; and said, 'that a quarrel between friends, when made up, added a new tie to friendship; *as experience shows that the callosity formed round a broken bone makes it stronger than before.* Those who are reconciled, often renew their friendship with increased warmth: *the offender is on his guard against a relapse, and anxious to atone for past unkindness; and the offended glory in forgiving and forgetting the wrongs that have been done to them.. Princes are doubly careful of reconquered towns, and preserve them with more care than those the enemy never gained.'*

"St. Francis had particular delight in contemplating a painting of the Penitent Magdalen at the Foot of the Cross, and sometimes called it his manual and his library. Seeing a copy of this picture at Bellay, 'Oh,' said he, 'what a blessed and advantageous exchange the penitent Mary made! She pours tears on the feet of Christ, and from those feet blood streams to wash away all her sins!' To this thought he added another: 'How carefully we should cherish *the little virtues which spring up at the foot of the cross,* since they are sprinkled with the blood of the Son of God!'

"'What virtues do you mean?' He replied, 'Humility, patience, meekness, benignity, bearing one another's burden, condescension, softness of heart, cheerfulness, cordiality, compassion, forgiving injuries, simplicity, candor; all, in short, of that sort. *They, like unobtrusive violets, love the shade;* like them, are sustained by dew; *and though, like them, they make little show, they shed a sweet odor on all around.*'

"To obey a ferocious, savage, ill-humored, thankless master, *is to draw clear water from a fountain streaming from the jaws of a brazen lion*, as Samson says. It is to find food in the devourer. It is to see *God only.*" [This is beautiful: and that is a fine bit of poetry about the lion; strength and sweetness meet in it. He is speaking of a master whom it happens to be incumbent on us to obey.]

"St. Francis highly esteemed those persons who kept inns, and entertained travellers,* provided they were civil and obliging; saying, that no condition in life, he thought, had greater means of serving God and man; for it is a continual exercise of benevolence and mercy, though, like a physician, the fee is paid."

[How oddly the following sounds in a Protestant ear, said of a "St. Francis"!]

"One day, after dinner, my friend was *amusing us with his entertaining conversation;* and, the subject

* The reader is to bear in mind that these were foreign inns, and in old times, when a tavern-keeper's life was not so easy as it is now.

of innkeepers being accidentally started, the different persons present very freely gave their opinions on the subject, and one among them declared the whole set to be rogues.

"This did not please St. Francis; but as it was *neither a fit time nor place for reproof*, nor was the sarcastic gentleman *in a mood to receive it*, he turned the discourse by telling the following anecdote: —

"'A Spanish pilgrim, little burdened with money, arrived at an inn, where, after having served him very ill, they charged him so much for his bad fare, that he loudly exclaimed at the injustice. However, being the weaker one, he was forced to give way and be satisfied. He left the inn in anger; and observing that it was facing another inn, and that in the intermediate space a cross had been erected, he soothed his rage by exclaiming, "Truly this place is a second Calvary, where the holy cross is stationed between two thieves" (meaning the two innkeepers). The host of the opposite hotel, without appearing to notice his displeasure, coolly asked what injury he had received from him, which he thus repaid with abuse. "Hush, hush," said the pilgrim, "my worthy friend; be not offended: you are *the good thief*. But what say you of your neighbor, who has flayed me alive?" This civility,' pursued St. Francis, 'soothed the pilgrim's wrath; but we should be careful not to stigmatize whole nations or trades by terming them rogues, impertinent, &c.; for, even if we have no individual in view, each individual of the nation or trade is a sufferer by the sarcasm, and cannot like to be so stigmatized.'

"To this I must add, that St. Francis so highly esteemed innkeepers, that, in travelling, he forbade his servants to dispute about their charges, and ordered them rather to pay than to expostulate; and when told that the bills were unreasonable, and that they asked more than they deserved, he would reply, 'What ought we to reckon in the account for their trouble, care, civility, and frequent disturbances at night? Certainly they cannot be too well paid.' This good-nature of my friend was so well known, that the innkeepers were always anxious to present their bills to him rather than to his servants; or else to throw themselves on his liberality, well knowing that he would give more than they could have asked."

POORNESS IN SPIRIT, AND SPIRIT IN POVERTY.

Of these we have two opposite examples in St. Charles Borromeo and St. Francis de Sales. St. Charles was nephew to the pope, and very wealthy: he had an income of more than a hundred thousand crowns, besides his considerable patrimony. But, amidst this wealth, he was poor in spirit: he had neither tapestry, plate, nor magnificent furniture. His table was so frugal as to be almost austere; and he himself lived chiefly on bread, water, and vegetables. The coffers which contained his treasures were the hands of the poor: thus in splendor was he humble.

Our saint had a different spirit: he was *rich in his poverty; of his bishopric little remained to him, and his patrimony he let his brothers enjoy.* But he never rejected tapestry, plate, nor fine furniture, especially what might adorn the altar; *for he loved to adorn the house of God.*

THOROUGH LOVE.

"We cannot deny that love is, of all mild emotions, the mildest, — the very sweetener of bitterness; yet we find it compared to death and the grave: the reason of which is, that nothing is so forcible as gentleness, and nothing so gentle and so amiable as firmness.

"There was a society of holy men," said St. Francis, "who one day accosted me thus: 'O sir! what can we do this year? Last year we failed, and did penance thrice a week: what shall we do now? Must we not do something more, both to testify our gratitude for the blessings we have received during the last year, and also that we may make some progress in the work of God?'

"'Very right,' I replied, 'that you should always be advancing: however, your progress will not be made by the methods you propose, — of increasing your religious exercises; but by the improved heart and dispositions with which you afford them, trusting in God more and more, and watching yourselves more and more. Last year, you fasted three days in each week: if you double the number of fasts this year, every day will be a day of abstinence; *and, the year following, what will you do? You will be obliged to make weeks of nine days long, or else to fast each day twice over.*'"

.[Here follows a strong and apparently a dangerous meat: yet the essence of sweetness, and even of safety, is in it. But pray ever mark our bold and admirable as well as amiable saint.]

"I do not know," said St. Francis, "how *that poor virtue, prudence*, has offended me; *but I cannot cordially like it:* I care for it *by necessity*, as being the salt and lamp of life. The beauty of simplicity charms me: *I would give a hundred serpents for one dove.* Both together, they are useful, and Scripture enjoins us to unite them: but as, in medical compounds, many drugs must be put together to form a salutary draught; so I would not place any reliance *on an equal dose;* for *the serpent might devour the inoffensive dove.* People say, that, in a corrupt age like the present, prudence is absolutely requisite to prevent being deceived. *I do not blame this maxim;* but I believe it is more Christian to let ourselves be devoured, and our goods spoiled, knowing that a better and more lasting inheritance awaits us. A good Christian would rather be robbed than rob others; rather be murdered than murderer, — martyred than tyrant: in a word, it is far better to be good and simple *than shrewd and mischievous.*

"There is a strange inconsistency in the human mind, which leads men to scrutinize with severity the secrets of their fellow-creatures' souls, *which it is impossible they should ever clearly discover;* while they neglect to examine and probe into the springs of their *own conduct*, which, if they *do not*, they certainly *ought to know.* The first they are forbidden, and the second they are commanded to do.

"This reminds me of a woman remarkable for her waywardness, and constant disobedience to the orders of her husband. She was drowned in a river. On hearing of it, her husband desired that the river should be dragged in search of the body: he bid his servants go *against* the current of the stream; observing, '*We have no reason to suppose that she should have lost her spirit of contradiction.*'"

St. Francis gave an excellent rule; which is, that "*if an action may be considered in more lights than one, always to choose the most favorable.* If there is no apology to be found, soften the bad impression it makes, by reflecting that the intention might not have been equally blamable: remember that the temptation might have been greater than you are aware of. Throw the odium on ignorance, carelessness, or the infirmity of human nature, to diminish the scandal.

"True devotion consists in performing the duties of life. St. Francis was in the habit of blaming an inconsistency very common in persons more than ordinarily devout, who frequently turn their attention to the attainment of *virtues of no use to them* in their own sphere of action, and neglect the more needful. This inconsistency he attributed to a distaste which people often experience for the station in which Providence has placed them, and the duties they are obliged to perform. Great laxity of manner creeps into monasteries, when their inmates devote themselves to the practice of virtues fitted for secular life; and errors are not less likely to make their way into private families, who, from a mistaken and ill-judged zeal, introduce among themselves the austerities and religious exercises of their secluded brethren.

"Some persons think they pronounce the highest eulogium in saying of a family who ought to perform the active charities of life, 'It is quite a monastery; they live in it like monks or nuns:' not reflecting that it is trying to find *figs on thorns, or grapes on brambles.*

"Not that exercises of piety are not right and good; but then the time, the place, the persons, the situation, in short, all circumstances, must be duly considered. Devotion misplaced ceases to be devotion: it resembles a fish out of water, or a tree in a soil not congenial to its nature.

"He compared this error of judgment, so unreasonable and injudicious, to those lovers of luxury who feed *on strawberries at Christmas*, not contented with delicacies in their proper season. *Such heated brains require the physician's discipline rather than the cool voice of sober reason.*"

AN ADMIRABLE RULE IN SELF-CORRECTION FOR MORBID OR VIOLENT CONSCIENCES.

"Since the degree of affection which we are commanded by God to feel for our neighbors ought to be measured by the reasonable and Christian love which we bear towards ourselves; since charity, which is benign and patient, obliges us to correct our neighbors for their failings with great gentleness,—*it does not appear right to alter that temper in correcting ourselves*, or to recover from a fault with feelings of bitter and intemperate displeasure."

SCALE OF VIRTUES.

"*First*, *St. Francis preferred the virtues most frequently called into action*, — *the commonest;* and to exercise which, opportunities are oftenest found.

"*Secondly*, He did not judge of the greatness and supernatural excellence of a virtue by an external demonstration: forasmuch as what appears a mere trifle may proceed from an exalted sentiment of charity and great assisting grace; while, on the contrary, great show may exist where the love of God operates but slightly, though that is the criterion by which we may judge whether or not a good work becomes acceptable to God.

"*Thirdly*, He preferred the virtues of more general influence rather than those more limited in their good effects (the love of God excepted). For example, he preferred prayer, as the star which gives light to every other excellence; piety, which sanctifies all our actions to the glory of God; humility, from which we have a lowly opinion of ourselves and our actions; meekness, which yields to the will of others; and patience, which teaches us to suffer all things; *rather* than magnanimity, munificence, or liberality; *because they embrace fewer objects*, *and their influence is less generally felt on the heart and temper.*

"*Fourthly*, He was often inclined to doubt the use of dazzling qualities, because by their brilliancy they gave an opening to vain-glory, the bane of all intrinsic worth.

"*Fifthly*, He blamed those who never set any value on virtues till they gained the sanction of fashion (a very bad judge of such merchandise) ; thus preferring ostensible to spiritual benevolence; fasting, penances, corporeal austerities, to gentleness, modesty, and self-government, *which are of infinitely more value.*

"*Sixthly*, He also reproved those who would not seek to obtain any virtues which were unsuited to their inclinations, to the neglect of what their duties more particularly required; serving God as it pleased themselves, and not in the manner which he commands. So common is this error, that a great number of persons, some very devout, suffer themselves to fall into it."

WE MAY BE VERY REGULAR IN DEVOTION, AND VERY WICKED.

"'Do not deceive yourself,' said my friend: 'it is not impossible to be very devout, and yet very wicked.'—'Very hypocritical,' I replied, 'and not sincerely pious.'—'*No: I speak of intentional devotion.*' This enigma appearing to me inexplicable, I begged he would explain his meaning more clearly. 'Devotion of self and of nature,' he answered, 'is only a morally acquired virtue, and not a heavenly one, assisted by grace: otherwise it would be theological, which certainly it is not. It is a quality subordinate to what is termed religion; or, as some say, it is only one of its effects, or fruits, *as religion is in itself subordinate to that one of the cardinal virtues called justice, or righteousness.*

"'You well know that all moral virtues, and also faith and hope, which are theological, may subsist with sin. They are then *without form or life, being deprived of* CHARITY, which is their substance, their soul, *and on which all their power depends.*'

"I lamented bitterly to St. Francis of the very hard treatment which I had received. 'To any other person,' he said, 'I should apply the unction of consolation; but the consideration of your situation in life, and the sincerity of my affection for you, render any such expression of affection needless. Pity would inflame the wound you have received. *I shall, therefore, throw vinegar and salt upon it.*'" [Is not this affected cruelty, and truly flattering candor, admirable?]

"'You said that it required amazing and well-tried patience to bear such an insult in silence.'

"'Certainly: yours cannot be of a very fine temperament, *since you complain so loudly.*'

"'But it is only in your friendly bosom, in the ear of your affection, that I pour out my sorrows. To whom should a child turn for compassion but to a kind parent?'

"'*Oh, you babe!* Is it fit, do you suppose, for one who occupies a lofty station in the Church of Christ, to encourage himself in such childishness? "When I was a child," said St. Paul, "I spake as a child; but, when I became a man, I put away childish things." *The imperfect articulation, so engaging in an infant, becomes an imperfection if continued in riper years.* Do you wish to be fed with milk and pap instead of solid food? Have you not *teeth* to masticate bread, EVEN THE BITTER BREAD OF GRIEF?

"'What! can you delight in bearing on your breast a golden cross, and then let your heart sink beneath the weight of slight affliction, and pour out bitter lamentations?'"

WE ARE APT TO GIVE THE NAME OF CALUMNY TO UNPLEASANT BUT WHOLESOME TRUTHS.

"Have patience with *all things*, but *chiefly* have patience with *yourself.* Do not lose courage in considering your own imperfections, but instantly set about remedying them: *every day, begin the task anew.* The best method of attaining to Christian perfection is to be aware that you have not yet reached it, but never to be weary of recommencing. For, in the first place, *how can you patiently bear your brother's burden, if you will not bear your own?*

"*Secondly*, How can you reprove any one with gentleness, when you correct yourself with asperity?

"*Thirdly*, Whosoever is overcome with a sense of his faults will not be able to subdue them: correction, to answer a good end, must proceed from a tranquil and thoughtful mind." He means a mind made tranquil by its own consciousness of good intention, and a mild consideration of what is best.

Erasmus said, that, when he considered the life and doctrines of Socrates, he was inclined to exclaim "*Sancte Socrates, ora pro nobis*" ("Saint Socrates, pray for us"); that is, to put him in the saintly and Christian calendar. We do not live under a Catholic dispensation; but certainly, while reading this book, we have been inclined to exclaim, "Would to God there were but one Christian Church, and such men as Saint Francis de Sales were counted saints by everybody,—not to be imitated by them in by-gone, ascetical customs, much less in opinions that must have perplexed such natures more than any others, but in the ever-living necessities of charity and good faith, and the hope that such a church may come! And it may, and we believe will; for utility itself will find it indispensable, to say nothing of those indestructible faculties of man that are necessary to render utility itself beautiful and useful. If earth is to be made smoother, most assuredly the sky cannot be left out of its consideration, nor will appear less lovely; and we never see an old quiet village church among the trees, under a calm heaven, — such as that, for instance, of Finchley or Hendon, — without feeling secure that such a time will arrive, with "Beauties" such as those of St. Francis de Sales preached in it, and congregations who have *really* discovered that "God is love."

THE EVE OF ST. AGNES.

THE reader should give us three pearls, instead of three half-pence,* for this number of our publication; for it presents him with the *whole* of Mr. Keats's beautiful poem, entitled as above, to say nothing of our loving commentary.

St. Agnes was a Roman virgin, who suffered martyrdom in the reign of Diocletian. Her parents, a few days after her decease, are said to have had a vision of her, surrounded by angels, and attended by a white lamb, which afterward became sacred to her. In the Catholic Church, formerly the nuns used to bring a couple of lambs to her altar during mass. The superstition is (for we believe it is still to be found), that, by taking certain measures of divination, damsels may get a sight of their future husbands in a dream. The ordinary process seems to have been by fasting. Aubrey (as quoted in "Brand's Popular Antiquities") mentions another; which is, to take a row of pins, and pull them out one by one, saying a Pater-noster; after which, upon going to bed, the dream is sure to ensue. Brand quotes Ben Jonson:—

* The price of the journal in which the article first appeared.

"And, on sweet St. Agnes' night,
Please you with the promised sight—
Some of husbands, some of lovers,
Which an empty dream discovers."

But another poet has now taken up the creed in good poetic earnest; and, if the superstition should go out in every other respect, in his rich and loving pages it will live for ever.

THE EVE OF ST. AGNES.

BY JOHN KEATS.

I.

St. Agnes' Eve.—Ah! bitter chill it was:
The owl, for all his feathers, was a-cold;
The hare limped trembling through the frozen grass,
And silent was the flock in woolly fold;
Numb were the beadsman's fingers while he told
His rosary, and while his frosted breath,
Like pious incense, from a censer old,
Seemed taking flight for heaven without a death,
Past the sweet Virgin's picture, while his prayer he saith.

What a complete feeling of winter-time is here, together with an intimation of those Catholic elegances of which we are to have more in the poem!

"The owl, with all his feathers, was a-cold."

Could he have selected an image more warm and comfortable in itself, and therefore better contradicted by the season? We feel the plump, feathery bird in his nook, shivering in spite of his natural household warmth, and staring out at the strange weather. The hare limping through the chill grass is very piteous, and the "silent flock" very patient; and how quiet and gentle, as well as winterly, are all these circumstances, and fit to open a quiet and gentle poem! The breath of the pilgrim, likened to "pious incense," completes them, and is a simile in admirable "keeping," as the painters call it; that is to say, is thoroughly harmonious in itself, and with all that is going on. The breath of the pilgrim is visible; so is that of a censer: his object is religious, and so is the use of the censer. The censer, after its fashion, may be said to pray; and its breath, like the pilgrim's, ascends to heaven. Young students of poetry may, in this image alone, see what imagination is, under one of its most poetical forms, and how thoroughly it "tells." There is no part of it unfitting. It is not applicable in one point, and the reverse in another.

II.

His prayer he saith, this patient, holy man;
Then takes his lamp, and riseth from his knees,
And back returneth, meagre, barefoot, wan,
Along the chapel aisle by slow degrees:
The sculptured dead on each side seemed to freeze,
Imprisoned in black purgatorial rails:
Knights, ladies, praying in dumb orat'ries,
He passeth by; and his weak spirit fails
To think how they may ache in icy hoods and mails.

The germ of this thought, or something like it, is in Dante; where he speaks of the figures that perform the part of sustaining columns in architecture. Keats had read Dante in Mr. Cary's translation, for which he had a great respect. He began to read him afterwards in Italian, which language he was mastering with surprising quickness. A friend of ours has a copy of Ariosto, containing admiring marks of his pen. But the same thought may have originally struck one poet as well as another. Perhaps there are few that have not felt something like it, in seeing the figures upon tombs. Here, however, for the first time, we believe, in English poetry, is it expressed, and with what feeling and elegance! Most wintry, as well as penitential, is the word "aching" in "icy hoods and mails," and most felicitous the introduction of the Catholic idea in the word "purgatorial." The very color of the rails is made to assume a meaning, and to shadow forth the gloom of the punishment,—

"*Imprisoned* in *black purgatorial* rails."

III.

Northward he turneth through a little door,
And scarce three steps, ere Music's golden tongue
Flattered to tears this aged man and poor:
But no; already had his death-bell rung;
The joys of all his life were said and sung:
His was harsh penance on St. Agnes' Eve:
Another way he went, and soon among
Rough ashes sat he, for his soul's reprieve;
And all night kept awake, for sinner's sake to grieve.

"*Flattered to tears* this aged man and poor."

This "flattered" is exquisite. A true poet is by nature a metaphysician; far greater in general than metaphysicians professed. He feels instinctively what the others get at by long searching. In this word "flattered" is the whole theory of the secret of tears; which are the tributes, more or less worthy, of self-pity to self-love. Whenever we shed tears, we take pity on ourselves; and we feel, if we do not consciously say so, that we deserve to have the pity taken. In many cases, the pity is just, and the self-love not to be construed unhandsomely. In many others, it is the reverse; and this is the reason why selfish people are so often found among the tear-shedders, and why they seem even to shed them for others. They imagine themselves in the situation of the others — as indeed the most generous must — before they can sympathize; but the generous console as well as weep. Selfish tears are niggardly of every thing but themselves.

"Flattered to tears." Yes, the poor old man was moved by the sweet music to think that so sweet a thing was intended for his comfort as well as for others. He felt that the mysterious kindness of Heaven did not omit even his poor, old, sorry case in its numerous workings and visitations; and, as he wished to live longer, he began to think that his wish was to be attended to. He began to consider how much he had suffered; how much he had suffered wrongly or mysteriously; and how much better a man he was, with all his sins, than fate seemed to have taken him for. Hence he found himself deserving of tears and self-pity; and he shed them, and felt soothed by his poor, old, loving self. Not undeservedly either; for he was a painstaking pilgrim, aged, patient, and humble, and willingly suffered cold and toil for the sake of something better than he could otherwise deserve; and so the pity is not exclusively on his own side: we pity him too, and would fain see him well out of that cold chapel, gathered into a warmer place than a grave. But it was not to be. We must, therefore, console ourselves with knowing that this icy endurance of his was the last, and that he soon found himself at the sunny gate of heaven.

IV.

That ancient beadsman heard the prelude soft;
And so it chanced (for many a door was wide
From hurry to and fro), soon up aloft
The *silver snarling trumpets* 'gan to chide;
The level chambers, ready with their pride,
Were glowing to receive a thousand guests:
The carved angels, ever eager-eyed,
Stared, where upon their heads the cornice rests,
With hair blown back, and wings put crosswise on their breasts.

V.

At length burst in the argent revelry,
With plume, tiara, and all rich array,
Numerous as shadows haunting fairily
The brain, new stuffed, in youth, with triumphs gay
Of old romance. These let us wish away,
And turn, sole-thoughted, to one Lady there,
Whose heart had brooded, all that wintry day,
On love, and winged St. Agnes' saintly care,
As she had heard old dames full many times declare.

VI.

They told her how, upon St. Agnes' Eve,
Young virgins might have visions of delight;
And soft adorings from their loves receive
Upon the honeyed middle of the night,
If ceremonies due they did aright:
As, supperless to bed they must retire,
And couch supine their beauties, lily white;
Nor look behind nor sideways, but require
Of Heaven with upward eyes for all that they desire.

VII.

Full of this whim was thoughtful Madeline:
The music, yearning like a god in pain,
She scarcely heard; her maiden eyes divine,
Fixed on the floor, saw many a sweeping train
Pass by, — she heeded not at all: in vain
Came many a tiptoe, amorous cavalier,
And back retired, not cooled by high disdain:
But she saw not; her heart was otherwhere;
She sighed for Agnes' dreams, the sweetest of the year.

VIII.

She danced along with vague, regardless eyes;
Anxious her lips, her breathing quick and short:
The hallowed hour was near at hand; she sighs
Amid the timbrels, and the thronged resort
Of whisperers, in anger or in sport;
'Mid looks of love, defiance, hate, and scorn;
Hood-winked with fairy fancy; all amort,
Save to St. Agnes and her lambs unshorn,
And all the bliss to be before to-morrow morn

IX.

So, purposing each moment to retire,
She lingered still. Meantime, across the moors,
Had come young Porphyro, with heart on fire
For Madeline. Beside the portal doors,
Buttressed from moonlight, stands he, and implores
All saints to give him sight of Madeline
But for one moment in the tedious hours,
That he might gaze, and worship all unseen;
Perchance speak, kneel, touch, kiss: in sooth, such things have been.

X.

He ventures in: let no buzzed whisper tell;
All eyes be muffled, or a hundred swords
Will storm his heart, Love's feverous citadel.
For him those chambers held barbarian hordes,

Hyena foemen, and hot-blooded lords,
Whose very dogs would execrations howl
Against his lineage. Not one breast affords
Him any mercy, in that mansion foul,
Save one old beldam weak in body and in soul,

XI.

Ah, happy chance! the aged creature came
Shuffling along with ivory-headed wand
To where he stood, hid from the torches' flame,
Behind a broad hall-pillar, far beyond
The sound of merriment and chorus bland.
He startled her: but soon she knew his face,
And grasped his fingers in her palsied hand;
Saying, "Mercy, Porphyro! hie thee from this place;
They are all here to-night, the whole bloodthirsty race.

XII.

"Get hence! get hence! There's dwarfish Hildebrand:
He had a fever late, and in the fit
He cursèd thee and thine, both house and land.
Then there's that old Lord Maurice, *not a whit*
More tame for his gray hairs. Alas, me! flit, —
Flit like a ghost away." — "Ah! gossip dear,
We're safe enough: here in this arm-chair sit,
And tell me how" — "Good saints! not here, not here!
Follow me, child, or else these stones will be thy bier."

XIII.

He followed through a lowly, archèd way,
Brushing the cobwebs with his lofty plume;
And as she muttered, "Well-a — well-a-day!"
He found him *in a little moonlight-room,*
Pale, latticed, chill, and silent as a tomb.
"Now tell me where is Madeline," said he:
"Oh! tell me, Angela, by the holy loom
Which none but secret Sisterhood may see,
When they St. Agnes' wool are weaving piously."

The poet does not make his "little moonlight-room" comfortable, observe. The high taste of the exordium is kept up. All is still wintry. There is to be no comfort in the poem but what is given by love. All else may be willingly left to the cold walls.

XIV.

"St. Agnes! Ah! it is St. Agnes' Eve;
Yet men will murder upon holy-days:
Thou must hold water in a witch's sieve,
And be the liege-lord of all elves and fays,
To venture so: it fills me with amaze
To see thee, Porphyro! — St. Agnes' Eve!
God's help! my lady fair the conjuror plays
This very night: good angels her deceive!
But let me laugh awhile; I've mickle time to grieve."

XV.

Feebly she laugheth in the languid moon,
While Porphyro upon her face doth look
Like puzzled urchin on an aged crone,
Who keepeth closed a wondrous riddle-book,
As spectacled she sits in chimney-nook:
But soon his eyes grew brilliant, when she told
His lady's purpose; and he scarce could brook
Tears at the thought of those enchantments cold,
And Madeline asleep in lap of legends old.

He almost shed tears of sympathy to think how his treasure is exposed to the cold, and of delight and pride to think of her sleeping beauty and her love for himself. This passage, "asleep in the lap of legends old," is in the highest imaginative taste; fusing together the tangible and the spiritual, the real and the fanciful, the remote and the near. Madeline is asleep in her bed; but she is also asleep in accordance with the legends of the season, and therefore the bed becomes *their* lap as well as sleep's. The poet does not critically think of all this; he feels it: and thus should other young poets draw upon the prominent points of their feelings on a subject, sucking the essence out of them into analogous words, instead of beating about the bush for *thoughts*, and perhaps getting very clever ones, but confused, — not the best, nor any one better than another. Such, at least, is the difference between the truest poetry and the degrees beneath it.

XVI.

Sudden a thought *came, like a full-blown rose,*
Flushing his brow, and in his painèd heart
Made purple riot: then doth he propose
A stratagem that makes the beldam start.
"A cruel man, and impious, thou art!
Sweet lady! let her pray and sleep and dream
Alone with her good angels, far apart
From wicked men like thee. Go, go! — I deem
Thou canst not, surely, be the same that thou dost seem."

XVII.

"I will not harm her, by all saints I swear!"
Quoth Porphyro: "oh! may I ne'er find grace,
When my weak voice shall whisper its last prayer,
If one of her soft ringlets I displace,
Or look with *ruffian-passion* in her face:
Good Angela, believe me, by these tears,
Or I will, even in a moment's space,
Awake with horrid shout my foemen's ears,
And beard them, though they be more fanged than wolves and bears."

XVIII.

"Ah! why wilt thou affright a feeble soul,—
A poor, weak, palsy-stricken, *churchyard* thing,
Whose passing-bell may ere the midnight toll;
Whose prayers for thee, each morn and evening,
Were never missed?" Thus, plaining, doth she bring
A gentler speech from burning Porphyro,
So woful, and of such deep sorrowing,
That Angela gives promise she will do
Whatever he shall wish, betide or weal or woe:

XIX.

Which was to lead him in close secrecy
Even to Madeline's chamber, and there hide
Him in a closet, of such privacy
That he might see her beauty unespied,
And win perhaps that night a peerless bride;
While legioned fairies paced the coverlet,
And pale enchantment held her sleepy-eyed.
Never on such a night have lovers met,
Since Merlin paid his demon all the monstrous debt.

What he means by Merlin's "monstrous debt" we cannot say. Merlin, the famous enchanter, obtained King Uther his interview with the fair Iogerne; but though he was the son of a devil, and conversant with the race, we are aware of no debt that he owed them.

XX.

"It shall be as thou wishest," said the dame;
"All cates and dainties shall be storèd there,
Quickly on this feast-night: by the tambour-frame
Her own lute thou wilt see. No time to spare;
For I am slow and feeble, and scarce dare
On such a catering trust my dizzy head.
Wait here, my child, with patience; kneel in prayer
The while: ah! thou must needs the lady wed;
Or may I never leave my grave among the dead!"

XXI.

So saying, she hobbled off with busy fear:
The lover's endless minutes slowly passed,
The dame returned, and whispered in his ear
To follow her; with aged eyes aghast
From fright of dim espial. Safe at last,
Through many a dusky gallery, they gain
The maiden's chamber, *silken, hushed, and chaste,*
Where Porphyro took covert, pleased amain:
His poor guide hurried back with agues in her brain.

XXII.

Her faltering hand upon the balustrade,
Old Angela was feeling for the stair,
When Madeline, St. Agnes' charmèd maid,
Rose, like a missioned spirit, unaware:
With silver taper's light, and pious care,
She turned, and down the aged gossip led
To a safe level matting. Now prepare,
Young Porphyro, for gazing on that bed:
She comes, she comes again, like ring-dove frayed and fled.

XXIII.

Out went the taper as she hurried in;
Its little smoke in pallid moonshine died:
She closed the door, she panted all akin
To spirits of the air, and visions wide;
Nor uttered syllable, or woe betide!
But to her heart her heart was voluble,
Paining with eloquence her balmy side;
As though a tongueless nightingale should swell
Her throat in vain, and die heart-stifled in her dell.

"Its little smoke in pallid moonshine died"—

is a verse in the taste of Chaucer, full of minute grace and truth. The smoke of the waxen taper seems almost as ethereal and fair as the moonlight, and both suit each other and the heroine. But what a lovely line is the seventh, about the heart—

"Paining with eloquence her balmy side"!

And the nightingale!—how touching the simile! the heart a "tongueless nightingale," dying in that dell of the bosom. What thorough sweetness, and perfection of lovely imagery! How one delicacy is heaped upon another! But for a burst of richness, noiseless, colored, suddenly enriching the moonlight, as if a door of heaven were opened, read the following:—

XXIV.

A casement, high and triple-arched, there was,
All garlanded with carven imageries
Of fruits and flowers, and bunches of knot-grass,
And diamonded with panes of quaint device,
Innumerable of stains and splendid dyes,
As are the tiger-moth's deep damasked wings;
And in the midst, 'mong thousand heraldries,
And TWILIGHT *saints, and dim emblazonings,*
A shielded 'scutcheon BLUSHED *with blood of queens and kings.*

Could all the pomp and graces of aristocracy, with Titian's and Raphael's aid to boot, go beyond the rich religion of this picture, with its "twilight saints," and its 'scutcheons "blushing with the blood of queens"? But we must not stop the reader:—

XXV.

Full on this casement shone the wintry moon,
And threw warm *gules* on Madeline's fair breast,
As down she knelt for Heaven's grace and boon;
Rose-bloom fell on her hands together prest,
And on her silver cross soft amethyst;
And on her hair a glory like a saint:
She seemed *a splendid angel, newly drest,*
Save wings, for heaven. Porphyro grew faint:
She knelt, so pure a thing, so free from mortal taint.

The lovely and innocent creature, thus praying under the gorgeous painted window, completes the exceeding and unique beauty of this picture, — one that will for ever stand by itself in poetry as an addition to the stock. It would have struck a glow on the face of Shakespeare himself. He might have put Imogen or Ophelia under such a shrine. How proper, as well as pretty, the heraldic term *gules*, considering the occasion! *Red* would not have been a fiftieth part so good. And with what elegant luxury he touches the "silver cross" with "amethyst," and the fair, human hands with "rose-color," the kin to their carnation! The lover's growing "faint" is one of the few inequalities which are to be found in the later productions of this great but young and over-sensitive poet. He had, at the time of writing his poems, the seeds of a mortal illness in him, and he doubtless wrote as he had felt; for he was also deeply in love, and extreme sensibility struggled in him with a great understanding. But our picture is not finished: —

XXVI.

Anon his heart revives: her vespers done,
Of all its wreathèd pearls her hair she frees;
Unclasps her *warmèd* jewels one by one;
Loosens her fragrant bodice; *by degrees*
Her rich attire creeps rustling to her knees:
Half-hidden, *like a mermaid in sea-weed,*
Pensive awhile she dreams awake, and sees
In fancy fair St. Agnes in her bed;
But dares not look behind, or all the charm is fled.

How true and cordial the "*warmèd* jewels"! and what matter of fact also, made elegant, is the rustling downward of the attire! and the mixture of dress and undress, and dishevelled hair, likened to a "mermaid in sea-weed"! But the next stanza is perhaps the most exquisite in the poem:—

XXVII.

Soon, trembling in her soft and chilly nest,
In sort of wakeful swoon, perplexed she lay,
Until the poppied warmth of sleep oppressed
Her soothèd limbs, and soul, fatigued away,
Flown, like a thought, until the morrow-day;
Blissfully havened both from joy and pain;
Clasped like a missal, where swart Paynims pray;
Blinded alike from sunshine and from rain,
AS THOUGH A ROSE SHOULD SHUT, AND BE A BUD AGAIN.

Can the beautiful go beyond this? We never saw it. And how the imagery rises!—"flown, like a *thought;*" "blissfully *havened;*" "clasped like a missal" in a land of *Pagans;* that is to say, where Christian prayer-books must not be seen, and are therefore doubly cherished for the danger. And then, although nothing can surpass the preciousness of this idea, is the idea of the beautiful, crowning all,—

"*Blinded* alike from sunshine and from rain,
As though a rose should shut, and be a bud again."

Thus it is that poetry, in its intense sympathy with creation, may be said to create anew, rendering its words almost as tangible as the objects they speak of, and individually more lasting; the spiritual perpetuity putting them on a level (not to speak it profanely) with the fugitive forms of the substance.

But we are to have more luxuries still, presently:—

XXVIII.

Stolen to this paradise, and so entranced,
Porphyro gazed upon her empty dress,
And listened to her breathing, if it chanced
To wake into a slumberous tenderness;
Which when he heard, that minute did he bless,
And breathed, himself; then from the closet crept,
Noiseless as fear in a wild wilderness,
And o'er the hushèd carpet silent stept,
And 'tween the curtains peeped, where, lo! how fast she slept.

XXIX.

Then by the bedside, where the faded moon
Made a dim silver twilight, soft he set
A table; and, half-anguished, threw thereon
A cloth of *woven crimson, gold and jet.*
Oh for some drowsy Morphean amulet!
The boisterous, midnight, festive clarion,
The kettle-drum, and far-heard clarionet,
Affray his ears, though but in dying tone:
The hall-door shuts again, and all the noise is gone.

XXX.

And still she slept *an azure-lidded sleep*
In blanchèd linen, smooth and lavendered;
While he from forth the closet brought a heap
Of candied apple, quince, and plum and gourd,
With jellies soother than the creamy curd,
And lucent sirups, tinct with cinnamon:
Manna and dates, in argosy transferred
From Fez; *and spicèd dainties, every one*
From silken Samarcand to cedared Lebanon.

Here is delicate modulation, and super-refined epicurean nicety!

"Lucent sirups, tinct with cinnamon,"

make us read the line delicately, and at the tip-end, as it were, of one's tongue.

XXXI.

These delicates he heaped with glowing hand
On golden dishes and in baskets bright
Of wreathèd silver: sumptuous they stand
In the retirèd quiet of the night,
Filling the chilly room with perfume light.
"And now, my love, my seraph fair, awake!
Thou art my heaven, and I thine eremite:
Open thine eyes, for meek St. Agnes' sake,
Or I shall drowse beside thee, so my soul doth ache."

XXXII.

Thus whispering, his warm, unnervèd arm
Sank in her pillow. Shaded was her dream
By the dusk curtains: 'twas a midnight charm
Impossible to melt as icèd stream:
The lustrous salvers in the moonlight gleam;
Broad golden fringe upon the carpet lies;
It seemed he never, never could redeem
From such a steadfast spell his lady's eyes;
So mused awhile, entoiled in woofèd phantasies.

XXXIII.

Awakening up, he took her hollow lute, —
Tumultuous, — and, in chords that tenderest be,
He played an ancient ditty, long since mute,
In Provence called "La belle dame sans mercy:"
Close to her ear touching the melody;
Wherewith disturbed she uttered a soft moan:
He ceased; she panted quick, and suddenly
Her blue affrayèd eyes wide open shone:
Upon his knees he sank, pale as smooth-sculptured stone.

XXXIV.

Her eyes were open, but she still beheld,
Now wide awake, the vision of her sleep:
There was a painful change, that nigh expelled
The blisses of her dream so pure and deep,

At which fair Madeline began to weep,
And moan forth witless words with many a sigh;
While still her gaze on Porphyro would keep,
Who knelt, with joinèd hands and piteous eye,
Fearing to move or speak, she looked so dreamingly.

XXXV.

"Ah, Porphyro!" said she, "but even now
Thy voice was a sweet tremble in mine ear,
Made tunable with every sweetest vow,
And those sad eyes were spiritual and clear:
How changed thou art! how pallid, chill, and drear!
Give me that voice again, my Porphyro,
Those looks immortal, those complainings dear:
Oh! leave me not in this eternal woe;
For if thou diest, my love, I know not where to go."

Madeline is half awake, and Porphyro re-assures her with living kind looks and an affectionate embrace.

XXXVI.

Beyond a mortal man impassioned far
At these voluptuous accents, he arose,
Ethereal, flushed, and like a throbbing star
Seen 'mid the sapphire heaven's deep repose:
Into her dream he melted, as the rose
Blendeth its odor with the violet,—
Solution sweet. Meanwhile the frost-wind blows
Like Love's alarum, pattering the sharp sleet
Against the window-panes: St. Agnes' moon hath set.

XXXVII.

'Tis dark; quick pattereth the flaw-blown sleet:
"This is no dream! my bride, my Madeline!"
'Tis dark: the icèd gusts still rave and beat.
"No dream, alas, alas! and woe is mine!
Porphyro will leave me here to fade and pine:
Cruel! what traitor could thee hither bring?
I curse not, for my heart is lost in thine,
Though thou forsakest a deceivèd thing,—
A dove, forlorn and lost, with sick unprunèd wing."

XXXVIII.

"My Madeline! sweet dreamer! lovely bride!
Say, may I be for aye thy vassal blest?
Thy beauty's shield, heart-shaped, and vermeil-dyed?
Ah! silver shrine, here will I take my rest,
After so many hours of toil and quest:
A famished pilgrim, saved by miracle,
Though I have found, I will not rob thy nest,
Saving of thy sweet self; if thou think'st well
To trust, fair Madeline, to no rude infidel."

With what a pretty wilful conceit the *costume* of the poem is kept up in the third line about the shield! The poet knew when to introduce apparent trifles forbidden to those who are void of real passion, and who, feeling nothing intensely, can intensify nothing.

XXXIX.

"Hark! 'tis an elfin-storm from Fairyland,
Of haggard seeming, but a boon indeed:
Arise, arise! the morning is at hand;
The bloated wassailers will never heed.
Let us away, my love! with happy speed:
There are no ears to hear, or eyes to see,—
Drowned all in Rhenish and the sleepy mead:
Awake, arise, my love! and fearless be;
For o'er the southern moors I have a home for thee."

XL.

She hurried at his words, beset with fears;
For there were sleeping dragons all around,
At glaring watch, perhaps, with ready spears;
Down the wide stairs a darkling way they found:
In all the house was heard no human sound.
A chain-drooped lamp was flickering by each door;
The arras, rife with horseman, hawk, and hound,
Fluttered in the besieging wind's uproar;
And the long carpets rose along the gusty floor.

This is a slip of the memory; for there were hardly carpets in those days. But the truth of the painting makes amends, as in the unchronological pictures of old masters.

XLI.

They glide, like phantoms, into the wide hall;
Like phantoms to the iron porch they glide,
Where lay the porter, in uneasy sprawl,
With a huge empty flagon by his side:
The wakeful blood-hound rose, and shook his hide,
But his sagacious eye an inmate owns;
By one and one, the bolts full easy slide;
The chains lie silent on the footworn stones;
The key turns, and the door upon its hinges groans.

XLII.

And they are gone: ay, ages long ago
These lovers fled away *into the storm.*
That night the baron dreamt of many a woe;
And all his warrior-guests, with shade and form
Of witch and demon, and large coffin-worm,
Were long be-nightmared. Angela the old
Died palsy-twitched, with meagre face deform;
The beadsman, after thousand aves told,
For aye unsought for slept among his ashes cold.

Here endeth the young and divine poet, but not the delight and gratitude of his readers; for, as he sings elsewhere, —

"A thing of beauty is a joy for ever."

A "NOW;"

Descriptive of a Cold Day.

"Now, all amid the rigors of the year."—THOMSON.

FRIEND tells us, that having written a "Now," descriptive of a hot day (see "Indicator"), we ought to write another, descriptive of a cold one; and accordingly we do so. It happens that we are, at this minute, in a state at once fit and unfit for the task; being in the condition of the little boy at school, who, when asked the Latin for "cold," said he had it "at his fingers' ends." But this helps us to set off with a right taste of our subject; and the fire, which is clicking in our ear, shall soon enable us to handle it comfortably in other respects.

Now, then, to commence. But, first, the reader who is good-natured enough to have a regard for these papers may choose to be told of the origin of the use of this word "Now," in case he is not already acquainted with it. It was suggested to us by the striking convenience it affords to descriptive writers, such as Thomson and others, who are fond of beginning their paragraphs with it, thereby saving themselves a world of trouble in bringing about a nicer conjunction of the various parts of their subject.

"*Now* when the first foul torrent of the brooks" —
"*Now* flaming up to heaven the potent sun" —
"*Now* when the cheerless empire of the sky" —
"But now" —
"When now" —
"Where now" —
"For now," — &c.

We say nothing of similar words among other nations, or of a certain *But* of the Greeks, which was as useful to them, on all occasions, as the *And so* of the little children's stories. Our business is with our old indigenous friend. No other *Now* can be so present, so instantaneous, so extremely *Now*, as our own Now. The now of the Latins — *Nunc*, or *Jam*, as he sometimes calls himself — is a fellow of past ages. He is no Now. And the *Nun* of the Greek is older. How can there be a *Now* which was *Then?* a "*Now-then,*" as we sometimes barbarously phrase it? "Now *and* then" is intelligible; but "Now-then" is an extravagance, fit only for the delicious moments of a gentleman about to crack his bottle, or to run away with a lady, or to open a dance, or to carve a turkey and chine, or to pelt snowballs, or to commit some other piece of ultra-vivacity, such as excuses a man from the nicer proprieties of language.

But to begin.

Now, the moment people wake in the morning, they perceive the coldness with their faces, though they are warm with their bodies, and exclaim, "Here's a day!" and pity the poor little sweep, and the boy with the water-cresses. How anybody can go to a cold ditch, and gather water-cresses, seems marvellous. Perhaps we hear great lumps in the street of something falling; and, looking through the window, perceive the roofs of the neighboring houses thick with snow. The breath is visible, issuing from the mouth as we lie. Now we hate getting up, and hate shaving, and hate the empty grate in one's bedroom; and water freezes in ewers, and you may set the towel upright on its own hardness; and the window-panes are frost-whitened, or it is foggy, and the sun sends a dull, brazen beam into one's room; or, if it is fine, the windows outside are stuck with icicles; or a detestable thaw has begun, and they drip: but, at all events, it is horribly cold, and delicate shavers fidget about their chambers, looking distressed, and cherish their hard-hearted enemy, the razor, in their bosoms, to warm him a little, and coax him into a consideration of their chins. Savage is a cut, and makes them think destiny really too hard.

Now breakfast is fine; and the fire seems to laugh at us as we enter the breakfast-room, and say, "Ha, ha! here's a better room than the bed-chamber!" and we always poke it before we do any thing else: and people grow selfish about seats near it; and little boys think their elders tyrannical for saying, "Oh! *you* don't want the fire; your blood is young!" And truly that is not the way of stating the case, albeit young blood is warmer than old. Now the butter is too hard to spread; and the rolls and toast are at their maximum; and the former look glorious as they issue smoking out of the flannel in which they come from the baker's; and people who come with single knocks at the door are pitied; and the voices of boys are loud in the street, sliding or throwing snow-balls; and the dustman's bell sounds cold; and we wonder how anybody can go about selling fish, especially with that hoarse voice; and schoolboys hate their slates, and blow their fingers, and detest infinitely the no-fire at school; and the parish-beadle's nose is redder than ever.

Now sounds in general are dull; and smoke out of chimneys looks warm and rich; and birds are pitied, hopping about for crumbs; and the trees look wiry and cheerless, albeit they are still beautiful to imaginative eyes, especially the evergreens, and the birch with boughs like dishevelled hair. Now mud in roads is stiff, and the kennel ices over, and boys make illegal slides in the pathways, and ashes are strewed before doors; or you crunch the snow as you tread, or kick mud-flakes before you, or are horribly muddy in cities.

But, if it is a hard frost, all the world is buttoned up and great-coated, except ostentatious elderly gentlemen, and pretended beggars with naked feet; and the delicious sound of "All hot!" is heard from roasted apple and potato stalls, the vender himself being cold, in spite of his "hot," and stamping up and down to warm his feet; and the little boys are astonished to think how he can eat bread and cold meat for his dinner, instead of the smoking apples.

Now skaters are on the alert; the cutlers' shop-windows abound with their swift shoes; and, as you approach the scene of action (pond or canal), you hear the dull grinding noise of the skates to and fro, and see tumbles, and Banbury cake-men and blackguard boys playing "hockey;" and ladies standing shivering on the banks, admiring anybody but their brother, especially the gentleman who is cutting figures of eight, who, for his part, is admiring his own figure. Beginners affect to laugh at their tumbles, but are terribly angry, and long to thump the by-standers. On thawing days, idlers persist to the last in skating or sliding amidst the slush and bending ice, making the Humane-Society-man ferocious. He feels as if he could give them the deaths from which it is his business to save them. When you have done skating, you come away feeling at once warm and numb in the feet, from the tight effect of the skates; and you carry them with an ostentatious air of indifference, as if you had done wonders; whereas you have fairly had three slips, and can barely achieve the inside edge.

Now riders look sharp, and horses seem brittle in the legs, and old gentlemen feel so; and coachmen, cabmen, and others, stand swinging their arms across at their sides to warm themselves; and blacksmiths'-shops look pleasant, and potato-shops detestable; the fishmongers' still more so. We wonder how he can live in that plash of wet and cold fish, without even a window. Now clerks in offices envy the one next the fireplace; and men from behind counters hardly think themselves repaid by being called out to speak to a countess in her chariot; and the wheezy and effeminate pastry-cook, hatless and aproned, and with his hand in his breeches-pockets (as the graphic Cruikshank noticeth in his almanac), stands outside his door, chilling his household warmth with attending to the ice which is brought him, and seeing it unloaded into his cellar like coals. Comfortable look the Miss Joneses, coming this way with their muffs and furs; and the baker pities the maid-servant cleaning the steps, who, for her part, says she is not cold, which he finds it difficult to believe.

Now dinner rejoiceth the gatherers together, and cold meat is despised; and the gout defieth the morrow, thinking it but reasonable on such a day to inflame itself with "t'other bottle;" and the sofa is wheeled round to the fire after dinner, and people proceed to burn their legs in their boots, and little boys their faces; and young ladies are tormented between the cold and their complexions; and their fingers freeze at the piano-forte; but they must not say so, because it will vex their poor comfortable grand-aunt, who is sitting with her knees in the fire, and who is so anxious that they should not be spoilt.

Now the muffin-bell soundeth sweetly in the streets, reminding us, not of the man, but his muffins, and of twilight and evening and curtains and the fireside. Now play-goers get cold feet; and invalids stop up every crevice in their rooms, and make themselves worse; and the streets are comparatively silent; and the wind rises and falls in moanings; and the fire burns blue and crackles; and an easy-chair, with your feet by it on a stool, the lamp or candles a little behind you, and an interesting book just opened where you left off, is a bit of heaven upon earth. People in cottages crowd close into the chimney, and tell stories of ghosts and murders; the blue flame affording something like evidence of the facts.

"The owl, with all her feathers, is a-cold,"*

or you think her so. The whole country feels like a petrifaction of slate and stillness, cut across by the wind; and nobody in the mail-coach is warm but the horses, who steam pitifully when they stop. The "oldest man" makes a point of never having "seen such weather." People have a painful doubt whether they have any chins or not; ears ache with the wind; and the wagoner, setting his teeth together, goes puckering up his cheeks, and thinking the time will never arrive when he shall get to the Five Bells.

At night, people become sleepy with the fireside, and long to go to bed, yet fear it on account of the different temperature of the bedroom; which is, furthermore, apt to wake them up. Warming-pans and hot-water bottles are in request; and naughty boys eschew their night-shirts, and go to bed in their socks.

"Yes," quoth a little boy to whom we read this passage, "and make their younger brother go to bed first."

* Keats, in the "Eve of St. Agnes." Mr. Keats gave us some touches in our account of the "Hot Day" (first published in the "Indicator"), as we sat writing it in his company, alas! how many years back! We have here made him contribute to our "Cold Day." This it is to have immortal friends, whose company never forsakes us.

ICE, WITH POETS UPON IT.

IT is related of an emperor of Morocco, that some unfortunate traveller having thought to get into his good graces by telling him of the wonders of other countries, and exciting, as he proceeded, more and more incredulity in the imperial mind, finished, as he imagined, his delightful climax of novelties, by telling him, that in his native land, at certain seasons of the year, people could walk and run upon the water; upon which such indignation seized his majesty, that, exclaiming, "Such a liar as this is not fit to live!" he whipped off the poor man's head with his cimeter.

It is a pity that some half-dozen captives had not been present, from other northern regions, to give the monarch's perplexity a more salutary turn, by testifying to similar phenomena: as, how you drove your chariot over the water; how lumps of water came rolling down hill like rocks; and how you chopped, not only your stone-hard meat, but your stone-hard drink; holding a pound of water between pincers, and pelting a fellow with a gill of brandy instead of a stone. For such things are in Russia and Tartary; where, furthermore, a man shall have half a yard of water for his beard; throw a liquid up in the air, and catch it a solid; and be employed in building houses made of water, for empresses to sit in and take supper. Catherine the Second had one: —

> "It was a miracle of rare device, —
> A sunny pleasure-dome, with caves of ice;"

thus realizing Mr. Coleridge's poetical description of the palace of Kubla Khan.

Many a natural phenomenon is as poetical as this, and adjusts itself into as imaginative shapes and lights. Fancy the meeting an island-mountain of green or blue ice, in a sunny sea, moving southwards, and shedding fountains from its sparkling sides! The poet has described the icicle, —

> "Quietly shining to the quiet moon;"

but the icicle (so to speak) described itself first to the poet. Water, when it begins to freeze, makes crystals of itself; the snow is all stars or feathers, or takes the shape of flowers upon your window; and the extreme of solemn grandeur, as well as of fairy elegance, is to be found in the operations of frost. In Switzerland, gulfs of petrified billows are formed in whole valleys by the descent of ice from the mountains, its alternate thawing and freezing, and the ministry of the wind. You stand upon a crag, and see before you wastes of icy solitude, looking like an ocean heaven-struck in the midst of its fury, and fixed for ever. Not another sight is to be seen but the ghastly white mountains that surround it; not a sound to be heard but of under-currents of water breaking away, or the thunders of falling ice-crags, or perhaps the scream of an eagle. 'Tis as if you saw the world before heat moved it, — the rough materials of the masonry of creation.

> "Far, far above, piercing the infinite sky,
> Mont Blanc appears, still, snowy, and serene, —
> Its subject-mountains their unearthly forms
> Pile round it, ice and rock; broad vales between
> Of frozen floods, unfathomable deeps,
> Blue as the overhanging heaven, that spread
> And wind among the accumulated steeps;
> A desert, peopled by the storms alone."
>
> SHELLEY.

On the other hand, what is more prettily beautiful than the snow above mentioned, or the hoar-frost upon the boughs of a tree, like the locks of Spenser's old man, —

> "As hoary frost with spangles doth attire
> The mossy branches of an oak half dead;"

or the spectacle (in the verses quoted below) of a Northern garden, —

> "Where through the ice the crimson berries glow"?

Our winters of late have been very mild; and most desirable is it, for the poor's sake, that they should continue so, if the physical good of the creation will allow it. But, when frost and ice come, we must make the best of them; and Nature, in her apparently severest operations, never works without some visible mixture of good, as well as a great deal of beauty (itself a good). Cold weather counteracts worse evils: the very petrifaction of the water furnishes a new ground for sport and pastime. Then, in every street, the little boys find a gliding pleasure; and the sheet of ice in the pond or river spreads a joyous floor for skaters. We touched upon this the other day in a "Now;" but *now* we have the satisfaction of being able to quote some fine verses of Mr. Wordsworth's on the subject, which we happened not to have by us at the moment. They are taken from a new edition of Mr. Hine's judicious and valuable "Selections" from that fine poet, just published by Mr. Moxon. They are the more interesting, inasmuch as they show Mr. Wordsworth to be a skater himself, — no mean reason for his being able to write so vigorously.

"SKATING.

"In the frosty season, when the sun
Was set, and, *visible for many a mile,*
The cottage windows through the twilight blazed,
I heeded not the summons. Happy time
It was indeed for all of us: for me
It was a time of rapture! Clear and loud
The village clock tolled six. I wheeled about,
Proud and exulting like an untired horse,
That cares not for his home. All shod with steel,
We hissed along the polished ice in games
Confederate, imitative of the chase
And woodland pleasures, — the resounding horn,
The pack loud bellowing, and the hunted hare.
So through the darkness and the cold we flew,
And not a voice was idle: with the din
Meanwhile the precipices rang aloud.
The leafless trees and every icy crag
Tinkled like iron; while the distant hills
Into the tumult sent *an alien sound*
Of melancholy, not unnoticed; while the stars
Eastward were sparkling clear, and in the west
The orange sky of evening died away.

Not seldom from the uproar I retired
Into a silent bay; or sportively
Glanced sideways, leaving the tumultuous throng,
To cut across the reflex of a star, —
Image, that, flying still before me, gleamed
Upon the glassy plain. And oftentimes,
When we had given our bodies to the wind,
And all the shadowy banks on either side
Came sweeping through the darkness, spinning still
The rapid line of motion, then at once
Have I, reclining back upon my heels,
Stopped short; yet still the solitary cliffs
Wheeled by me, even as if the earth had rolled
With visible motion her diurnal round!
Behind me did they stretch in solemn train,
Feebler and feebler; and I stood and watched
Till all was tranquil as a summer sea."

Better for great poets to write in this manner, and show Nature's kindliness in the midst of what might seem otherwise, than to do as Dante and Milton have done, and add the tortures of frost and ice to the horrors of superstition. Be never their names, however, mentioned without reverence. The progress of things may have required at their hands what we can smile at now as a harmless terror of poetry. With what fine solid lines Milton always "builds" his verse! —

"Beyond this flood* a frozen continent
Lies dark and wild, beat with perpetual storms
Of whirlwind and dire hail, which on firm land
Thaws not, but gathers heap, and ruin seems
Of ancient pile, or else deep snow and ice, —

---

* The river of Oblivion.

A gulf profound, as that Serbonian bog
Betwixt Damiata and Mount Casius old,
Where armies whole have sunk.* The parching air
Burns frore, and cold performs the effect of fire.
Thither, by harpy-footed furies haled,
At certain revolutions, all the damned
Are brought, and feel by turns the bitter change
Of fierce extremes, extremes by change more fierce
From beds of raging fire, to starve in ice
Their soft ethereal warmth, and there to pine
Immovable, infixed, and frozen round,
Periods of time, thence hurried back to fire." †

---

* "Serbonis," says Hume (not the historian, but the commentator on Milton), "was a lake of two hundred furlongs in length and a thousand in compass, between the ancient mountain Casius and Damiata, a city of Egypt, on one of the more eastern mouths of the Nile. It was surrounded on all sides by hills of loose sand, which, carried into the water by high winds, so thickened the lake, as not to be distinguished from part of the continent, where whole armies have been swallowed up. Read 'Herodotus,' lib. iii., and Lucan's 'Pharsalia,' viii. 539, &c." — *Todd's edition of Milton*, vol. ii. p. 47.

† We add another note or two from Mr. Todd's "Milton," to show what pleasant reading there is in these Variorum editions, and to recommend them to more general attention. A great poet cannot be too thoroughly studied: —

"This circumstance of the damned suffering the extremes of heat and cold by turns seems to be founded upon Job xxiv. 19; not as it is in the English translation, but in the vulgar Latin version, which Milton often used: 'Ad *nimium calorem* transeat ab *aquis nivium*,' — 'Let him pass to *excessive heat* from *waters of snow*.' And so Jerome and other commentators understand it. The same punishments after death are mentioned by Shakespeare, 'Measure for Measure,' act iii. sc. i.: —

'And the delighted spirit
To bathe in fiery floods, or to reside
In thrilling regions of thick-ribbed *ice*.'"

BISHOP NEWTON.

"This circumstance of the damned's feeling the fierce extremes is also in Dante, 'Inferno,' c. iii. 86: —

We will take the taste of the bitter-cold barbarity of this passage out of the reader's heart by plunging him into the "warm South," with its good-natured sunshine; where, when he has basked enough in some noon of heat, vine-leaves, and brown laughing faces, so as to make the idea of cold pleasant to him again, and his eye turn wistfully to those snow-topped mountains yonder, cooling the blue burning air, let him refresh his wine with the Bacchus of the Italian poet Redi: —

ICE NECESSARY TO WINE.

Col topazio pigiato in Lamporecchio,
Ch' è famoso Castel per quel Masetto,
A inghirlandar le tazze or m' apparecchio,
Purchè gelato sia, e sia puretto,
Gelato, quale alla stagion del' gielo
Il più freddo Aquilon fischia pel cielo.

'I' vengo per menarvi all' altra riva
Nelle tenebre eterne, in caldo e'n *gielo*.'

'I come to lead thee to the other shore
Of the eternal glooms, through heat and ice.'

See also the 'Purgatorio,' c. iii. 31. So in 'Songs and Sonnets,' by Lord Surrey and others, 1587, fol. 83: —

'The soules that lacked grace,
Which lie in bitter pain,
Are not in such a place
As foolish folk do fayne:
Tormented all with fire,
And boyle in lead again;
Then cast *in frozen pits*
To *frese* there certain hours.'

And in Heywood's 'Hierarchie of Angels,' 1635, p. 345: —

'And suffer as they sinned, in wrath, *in paines*
Of frosts, of fires, of furies, whips, and chains.'

"In the preceding quotation from Surrey's 'Songs and Sonnets,' there is evidently a sneer at the monks, from whose legendary hell, according to Mr. Warton, the punishment by cold derives its origin." — TODD.

Cantinette e cantimplore
Stieno in pronto a tutte l' ore
Con forbite bombolette
Chiuse e strette tra le brine
Delle nevi cristalline.
Son le nevi il quinto elemento
Che compongono il vero bevere:
Ben è folle chi spera ricevere
Senza nevi nel bere un contento:
Venga pur da Valombrosa
Neve a josa;
Venga pur da ogni bicocca
Neve in chiocca;
E voi, Satiri, lasciate
Tante frottole, e tanti riboboli,
E del ghiaccio mi portate
Da la grotta del Monte di Boboli.
Con alti picchi
De' mazzapicchi
Dirompetelo,
Sgretolatelo,
Infragnetelo,
Stritolatelo,
Finchè tutto si possa risolvere
In minuta freddissima polvere,
Che mi renda il ber più fresco
Per rinfresco del palato,
Or ch' io son mortoassetato.

Bacco in Toscana.

"You know Lamporecchio, the castle renowned
For the gardener so dumb, whose works did abound:
There's a topaz they make there; pray, let it go round.
Serve, serve me a dozen;
But let it be frozen, —
Let it be frozen and finished with ice;
And see that the ice be as virginly nice
As the coldest that whistles from wintry skies.

Coolers and cellarets, crystal with snows,
Should always hold bottles in ready repose.
Snow is good liquor's fifth element;
No compound without it can give content:
For weak is the brain, and I hereby scout it,
That thinks in hot weather to drink without it
Bring me heaps from the Shady Valley;*
Bring me heaps
Of all that sleeps
On every village hill and alley.
Hold there, you satyrs,
Your beard-shaking chatters!
And bring me ice duly, and bring it me doubly,
Out of the Grotto of Monte di Boboli.
With axes and pickaxes,
Hammers and rammers,
Thump it and hit it me,
    Crack it and crash it me,
Hew it and split it me,
    Pound it and smash it me,
Till the whole mass (for I'm dead-dry, I think)
Turns to a cold, fit to freshen my drink."

Ice is such a luxury in the south of Europe, and has become also such a necessity, that, in some places, a dearth of it is considered the next thing to a want of bread. To preach tortures of ice at Naples would be the counterpart of the mistake of the worthy missionary, who was warned how he said too much of the reverse kind of punishment to the Laplanders. Dante was a native of Florence, where they have winters hard enough; and where, by the way, during its delightful summers, we have eaten, for a few pence,

* Valombrosa, which an Englishman may call *Milton's* Valombrosa. The convent is as old as the time of Ariosto, who celebrates the monks for their hospitality.

ice-cream enough to fill three of our silver-costing glasses in England. They bring it you in goblets. The most refreshing beverage we ever drank was a Florentine lemonade, made with fresh lemons (off the tree), sweetened with capillaire, and floating with ice.

But, if it were not for our subject, we ought to keep these summer reminiscences for next August. We conclude with a proper winter picture, painted by one who has been thought (and *is*, compared with great ones) a very small poet (Ambrose Philips), but who had a vein of truth in all he wrote, which would have obtained him more esteem in an age of poets than it did in an age of wits. Good-natured Steele, however, discerned his merits; and the poem before us, which Steele inserted in the "Tatler," was admired by them all. It was too new in its localities, and too evidently drawn from nature, not to please them; and was furthermore addressed to and patronized by a wit, — the Earl of Dorset.

A NORTHERN WINTER.

COPENHAGEN, *March* 9, 1709.

From frozen climes, and endless tracts of snow,
From streams that northern winds forbid to flow,
What present shall the Muse to Dorset bring,
Or how so near the Pole attempt to sing?
The hoary winter here conceals from sight
All pleasing objects that to verse invite.
The hills and dales and the delightful woods,
The flowery plains and silver-streaming floods,
By snow disguised, in bright confusion lie,
And with one dazzling waste fatigue the eye.
  No gentle-breathing breeze prepares the spring,
Nor birds within the desert region sing.

The ships, unmoved, the boisterous winds defy,
While rattling chariots o'er the ocean fly.
The vast Leviathan wants room to play,
And spout his waters in the face of day;
The starving wolves along the main sea prowl,
And to the moon in icy valleys howl.
For many a shining league, the level main
Here spreads itself into a glassy plain:
There solid billows of enormous size,
Alps of green ice, in wild disorder rise.
  And yet, but lately have I seen, even here,
The winter in a lovely dress appear:
Ere yet the clouds let fall the treasured snow,
Or winds began through hazy skies to blow,
At evening a keen eastern breeze arose,
And the descending rain unsullied froze.
Soon as the silent shades of night withdrew,
The ruddy morn disclosed at once to view
The face of Nature in a rich disguise,
And brightened every object to my eyes;
For every shrub, and every blade of grass,
And every pointed thorn, seemed wrought in glass.
In pearls and rubies rich the hawthorns show,
While through the ice the crimson berries glow.
The thick-sprung reeds the watery marshes yield
Seem polished lances in a hostile field.
The stag in limpid currents, with surprise,
Sees crystal branches on his forehead rise.
The spreading oak, the beech, and towering pine,
Glazed over, in the freezing ether shine.
The frighted birds the rattling branches shun,
That wave and glitter in the distant sun.
When, if a sudden gust of wind arise,
The brittle forest into atoms flies;
The crackling wood beneath the tempest bends,
And in a spangled shower the prospect ends;
Or if a southern gale the region warm,
And by degrees unbind the wintry charm,

The traveller a miry country sees,
And journeys sad beneath the dripping trees.
Like some deluded peasant, Merlin leads
Through fragrant bowers and through delicious meads;
While here enchanted gardens to him rise,
And airy fabrics there attract his eyes,
His wandering feet the magic paths pursue;
And, while he thinks the fair illusion true,
The trackless scenes disperse in fluid air,
And woods and wilds and thorny ways appear:
A tedious road the weary wretch returns,
And, as he goes, the transient vision mourns.

THE PIANO-FORTE.

HENRY THE FOURTH expressed a patriotic hope to see the time arrive when every man in France should have "a fowl boiling in his pot." The anathemas of an able political writer* against music-playing in farmers' houses (very just, if his calculation of the effect of it were the only one) do not hinder us from expressing a hope, that the time may arrive when every family that can earn its subsistence shall have its piano-forte; not to make them "fine and fashionable," or contemptuous of any right thinking, but to help them to the pleasures of true refinement, to reward them for right thinking and right doing, and make them feel how compatible are the homeliest of their duties with an elegant recreation,—just as the fields and homesteads around them are powdered with daisies and roses, and the very cabbages in their gardens can glitter with sunny dewdrops, to those that have eyes beyond their common use.

In Germany, they have piano-fortes in inns and cottages: why should they not have them in England? The only true answer is, Because we seafaring and commercial Saxons, by very reason of our wealth, and of the unequal advance of knowledge in comparison

* Mr. Cobbett.

with it, have missed the wiser conclusions, in this respect, of our Continental brethren, and been accustomed to the vulgar mistake of identifying all refinement with riches, and consequently all the right of being refined with the attainment of them. We fancy that nobody can or will be industrious, and condescend to a homely duty, who has a taste for an elegance; and, so fancying, we bring up the nation, at their peril, to have the same opinion; and thus the error is maintained, and all classes suffer for it, — the rich, because it renders them but half sensible of the real enjoyment of their accomplishments, and makes them objects of jealousy to the poor; and the poor, because it forces them to work out, with double pain, that progression towards a better state of things, the steps of which would be healed and elevated by such balmy accompaniments. In England, it is taken for an affectation, or some worse sign, if people show an inclination to accomplishments not usually found within their sphere. But the whole evil consists in the accomplishments not being there already, and constituting a part of their habits: for, in Germany, the circumstance is regarded with no such ill-will; nor do the male or female performers who can play on the piano-forte, or sing to it (and there are millions of such), fancy they have the fewer duties to perform, or that they are entitled a bit the more to disrespect those duties. On the contrary, they just know so much the better what is good both in the duty and the recreation: for no true thing can co-exist falsely with another that is true; each reflects light and comfort on each. To have one set of feelings harmonized, and put in good key, is to enable us to turn others to their best account; and he or she who could go from their music to their duties in a frame of mind the worse for it would only be the victim of a false opinion eradicable, and not of a natural feeling improvable. But false refinements are first set up, and then made judges of true ones. A foolish rich man, who can have concerts in his house, identifies his music, not with any thing that he really feels or knows about it, but with his power to afford it. He is of opinion with *Hugh Rebeck*, in the play, when he is asked why music is said to have a "silver sound:" "Because musicians sound for silver." But, if he knew what music really was, he would not care twopence for the show and flare of the thing, any more than he would to have a nightingale painted like a parrot. You may have an Æolian harp in your window, that shall cost twenty guineas: you may have another that shall cost little more than as many pence. Will the winds visit the poor one with less love, or the true ear hear it with the less rapture? One of the obstacles in the way of a general love of music, in this country, is the dearness of it, both print and instrument; and this is another effect of the mistakes of wealth. The rich, having monopolized music, have made it costly; and the mistaken spirit of trade encourages the delusion, instead of throwing open the source of comfort to greater numbers. A costly piano-forte makes a very fine, and, it must be owned, a very pleasing show in a room, if made in good taste; but not a bit of the fineness is necessary to it. A piano-forte is a harp in a box; and the box might be made of any decent materials, and the harp strung for a comparative nothing to what it is now. If we took a lesson from our cousins in Saxony and Bavaria, the demand for cheap piano-fortes would soon bring down the price; and instead of quarrelling over their troubles, or muddling them with beer and opium, and rendering themselves alike unfit for patience and for action, the poor would "get up" some music in their villages, and pursue their duties or their claims with a calmness beneficial to everybody.

We are aware of the political question that might be put to us at these points of our speculation; but we hold it to be answered by the real nature of the case, and, in fact, to have nothing whatever to do with it. We are an unmusical people at present (unless the climate have to do with it), simply because of what has been stated, and not for any reason connected with questions of greater or less freedom. The most musical countries — Greece, Italy, and Germany — have alike been free or enslaved, according as *other* circumstances happened, not as music was more or less regarded; with this difference, that the more diffused the music, the more happy the peace, or the more "deliberate" the "valor."* The greatest

* "Anon they move
In perfect phalanx to the Dorian mood
Of flutes and soft recorders, such as raised
To height of noblest temper heroes old
Arming to battle; and, instead of rage,
Deliberate valor breathed, firm and unmoved,
With dread of death to flight or foul retreat:
Nor wanting power to mitigate and 'swage
With solemn touches troubled thought, and chase
Anguish and doubt and fear and sorrow and pain
From mortal or immortal minds." — *Paradise Lost.*

among the most active as well as most contemplative of mankind have been lovers of music, often performers of it; and have generally united, in consequence, both action and contemplation. Epaminondas was a flute-player; so was Frederick the Second; and Luther and Milton were organists.

In connection with music, then, let us hear nothing about politics, either way. It is one of God's goods which we ought to be desirous to see cultivated among us, next after corn and honesty and books. The human hand was made to play it, the ear to hear it, the soul to think it something heavenly; and, if we do not avail ourselves of it accordingly, we turn not our hands, ears, and souls to their just account, nor reap half the benefit we might from the very air that sounds it.

A piano-forte is a most agreeable object. It is a piece of furniture with a soul in it, ready to waken at a touch, and charm us with invisible beauty. Open or shut, it is pleasant to look at; but, open, it looks best, smiling at us with its ivory keys, like the mouth of a sweet singer. The keys of a piano-forte are of themselves an agreeable spectacle, — an elegance not sufficiently prized for their aspect, because they are so common; but well worth regarding even in that respect. The color of the white keys is not a cold white; or, even when at their whitest, there is something of a warmth in the idea of ivory. The black furnish a sort of tessellation, and all are smooth and easy to the touch. It is one of the advantages of this instrument to the learner, that there is no discord to go through in getting at a tone. The tone is ready made. The finger touches the key, and there is music at once. Another and greater advantage is, that it contains a whole concert in itself; for you may play with all your fingers, and then every finger performs the part of a separate instrument. True, it will not compare with a real concert, — with the rising winds of an orchestra: but in no single instrument, except the organ, can you have such a combination of sounds; and the organ itself cannot do for you what the piano-forte does. You can neither get it so cheap, nor will it condescend to play every thing for you as the other does. It is a lion which has "no skill in dandling the kid." It is a Jupiter, unable to put off his deity when he visits you. The piano-forte is not incapable of the grandest music; and it performs the light and neat to admiration, and does not omit even the tender. You may accompany with it, almost equally well, the social graces of Mozart, and the pathos of Winter and Paesiello; and as to a certain miniature brilliancy of taste and execution, it has given rise to a music of its own, in the hands of Clementi and others. All those delicate ivory keys, which repose in such evenness and quiet, wait only the touch of the master's fingers to become a dancing and singing multitude, and, out of apparent confusion, make accordant loveliness. How pleasant to the uninitiated to see him lay his hand upon them, as if in mere indifference or at random; and, as he dimples the instrument with touches wide and numerous as rain-drops on a summer sea, play upon the ear the most regular harmonies, and give us, in a twinkling, elaborations which it would take us years to pick out! We forget that he has gone through the same labor, and think only of the beautiful and mysterious result. He must have a taste, to be sure, which no labor can gift him with; and of this we have a due sense. We wish we had a book by us, written a few years back, entitled "A Ramble among the Musicians in Germany," in order that we might quote a passage from it about the extempore playing of Hummel, the celebrated master who was lately in this country: but, if we are not mistaken, it is the hand of the same writer, which in so good a style, between sport and scholarship, *plays* its musical criticisms every week in "The Atlas;" for they are the next thing to an instrument themselves; and we recommend our readers to get a sight of that paper as often as they can, in order to cultivate the taste of which England at present seems to be so promisingly ambitious. By the way, we know not whether the Italians use the word in the same sense at present; but, in an old dictionary in our possession, the keys of musical instruments are called "tasti," — *tastes*, — a very expressive designation. You do *taste* the piano-forte the moment you touch it. Anybody can taste it; which, as we said before, is not the case with other instruments, the tone in them not being ready-made; though a master, of course, may apply the word to any.

> "So said, his hand, sprightly as fire, he flings,
> And with a quavering coyness *tastes* the strings."

There are superfine ears that profess not to be able to endure a piano-forte after a concert; others that always find it to be out of tune; and more who veil their insensibility to music in general, by protesting against "everlasting tinkles" and school-girl affectation or sullenness. It is not a pleasure, certainly, which a man would select, to be obliged to witness affectations of any sort, much less sullenness or any other absurdity. Such young ladies as are perpetually thinking of their abstract pretensions, and either affectedly trying to screw up their musical skill to them, or resenting, with tears and petty exclamations, that they cannot do it, are not the most sensible and agreeable of all possible charmers. But these terrible calamities may be safely left to the endurance or non-endurance of the no less terrible critics, who are so merciless upon them, or pretend to be. The critics and the performers will equally take themselves for prodigious people; and music will do both parties more good than harm in the long-run, however their zeal may fall short of their would-be capacity for it. With respect to piano-fortes not perfectly in tune, it is a curious fact in the history of sounds, that no instrument is ever perfectly in tune. Even the heavenly charmer, Music, being partly of earth as well as of heaven, partakes the common imperfection of things sublunary. It is therefore possible to have senses too fine for it, if we are to be always sensible of this imperfection; to —

"Die of an *air* in *achromatic* pain;"

and, if we are not to be thus sensible, who is to judge at what nice point of imperfection the disgust is to begin, where no disgust is felt by the general ear? The sound of a trumpet, in Mozart's infancy, is said to have threatened him with convulsions. To such a man, and especially to so great a master, every right of a horror of discord would be conceded, supposing his ear to have grown up as it began; but that it did not do so, is manifest from his use of trumpets; while, at the same time, so fine *beyond* ultra-fineness was his ear, that there is a passage in his works, pronounced impracticably discordant by the whole musical world, which nevertheless the critics are agreed that he must have written as it stands.* In other words, Mozart perceived a harmony in discord itself, or what universally appeared to be such, — just as very fine tastes in eating and drinking relish something which is disliked by the common palate; or as the reading world discovered, not long ago, that Pope, for all his sweetness, was not so musical a versifier as those "crabbed old English poets." The crabs were found to be very apples of the Hesperides. What we would infer from this is, that the same exquisite perception which discerned the sweetness in the sour of that discord would not have been among the first to despise an imperfection in the tuning of an instrument; nor, though he might wish it away, be rendered insensible by it of that finest part of the good music it performed, which consists in invention and expression and grace, — always the flower of music, as of every other art; and to be seen and enjoyed by the *very* finest ears as well as the humbler ones of good-will, because the soul of a thing is worth more to them than the body of it, and the greater is greater than the less.

Thus much to caution true lovers of music how they

* We cannot refer to it in its place; but it was quoted some time since in "The Atlas."

suffer their natural discernment to be warped by niceties, "more nice than wise;" and to encourage them, if an instrument pleases the general lovers of music, to try and be pleased with it as much as they can themselves, maugre what technical refiners may say of it, probably out of a jealousy of those whose refinements are of a higher order. *All* instruments are out of tune, the acoustic philosopher tells us. Well, be it so; provided we are not so much out of tune ourselves as to know it, or to be unable to discern something better in spite of it.

As to those who, notwithstanding their pretended love of music at other times, are so ready to talk of "jingling" and "tinkling" whenever they hear a piano-forte or a poor girl at her lesson, they have really no love of music whatsoever, and only proclaim as much to those who understand them. They are among the wiseacres, who are always proving their spleen at the expense of their wit.

Piano-fortes will probably be much improved by the next generation. Experiments are daily making with them, sometimes of much promise; and the extension of science on all hands bids fair to improve whatever is connected with mechanism. We are very well content, however, for ourselves, with the instrument as it is; are grateful for it, as a concert in miniature; and admire it as a piece of furniture in all its shapes: only we do not like to see it made a table of, and laden with movables; nor, when it is upright, does it seem quite finished without a bust on it; perhaps because it makes so good a pedestal, and seems to call for one.

Piano-forte (soft and strong) is not a good name for an instrument which is no softer nor stronger than some others. The organ unites the two qualities most; but *organ* (οργανον, *instrumentum*, — as if *the instrument*, by excellence) is the proper word for it; not to be parted with, and of a sound fit for its nobleness. The word "piano-forte" came up, when the harpsichord and spinet, its predecessors, were made softer. *Harpsichord* (arpichorda, — commonly called in Italian clavicembalo, or keyed cymbal, *i.e.* a box, or hollow, *Fr.* clavecin) is a sounding, but hardly a good word; meaning a harp with chords, — which may be said of any harp. *Spinet*, an older term (*spinette*, "thorns"), signifies the quills which used to occupy the place of the modern clothed hammers, and which produced the harsh sound in the old instruments; the quill striking the edge of the strings, like the nicking of a guitar-string by the nail. The spinet was preceded by the *virginals;* the oldest instrument, we believe, of the kind, — so called, perhaps, from its being chiefly played upon by young women, or because it was used in singing hymns to the Virgin. Spenser has mentioned it in an English *trimeter-iambic;* one of those fantastic attempts to introduce the uncongenialities of Latin versification, which the taste of the great poet soon led him to abandon. The line, however, in which the virginals are mentioned, presents a picture not unworthy of him. His apostrophe, at the outset, to his "unhappie verse," contains an involuntary satire: —

> "*Unhappie Verse,* the witnesse of my unhappie state!
> Make thyself fluttering wings of thy fast-flying

Thought, and fly forth unto my Love whersoever she be;
Whether lying restless in heavy bedde, or else
Sitting so cheerelesse at the cheerfull boarde, or else
Playing alone carelesse on her heavenlie virginals."

Queen Elizabeth is on record as having played on the virginals. It has been supposed by some that the instrument took its name from her; but it is probably older. The musical instrument mentioned in one of Shakespeare's sonnets is of the same keyed family. What a complete feeling of the *andante*, or *going* movement (as the Italians call it), is there in the beautiful line which we have marked! and what a pleasant mixture of tenderness and archness throughout!

"How oft when thou, my music, music play'st
Upon that blessed wood, whose motion sounds
With thy sweet fingers, when thou gently sway'st
The wiry concord that mine ear confounds,
Do I envy those jacks, that nimble leap
To kiss the tender inward of thy hand,
Whilst my poor lips, that should that harvest reap,
At the wood's boldness by thee blushing stand!
To be so tickled, they would change their state
And situation with those dancing chips
O'er whom thy fingers walk with gentle gait!
Since saucy jacks so happy are in this,
Give them thy fingers, me thy lips, to kiss."

Thus we have two out of our great poets, Spenser and Shakespeare, showing us the delight they took in the same species of instrument which we have now, and so bringing themselves near to our piano-fortes.

"Still virginalling
Upon his palm,"

says the jealous husband in the "Winter's Tale." Chaucer, Spenser, Shakespeare, and Milton, all mention the organ. Chaucer speaks of several instruments; but we cannot trace to him any other keyed one. It is rather surprising that the poets, considering the love of music natural to them, and their frequent mention of the art, have spoken of so few musical instruments; at least, as if conversant with them in their houses. Milton was an organ-player, and Gay a flute-player, (how like the difference of their genius!) Thomson possessed an Æolian harp, of which he seems to have been very fond. He has addressed an ode to it (from which the verses have been set to music, beginning,—

"Methinks I hear the full celestial choir");

and has again mentioned the instrument in his "Castle of Indolence,"—a most fit place for it.

All the truest lovers of any one art admire the other arts. Farinelli had several harpsichords, to which he gave the names of painters, according to their respective qualities,—calling one his Raphael, another his Correggio, &c. And the exquisite little painting, by Annibal Carracci, in the British Gallery, of "Silenus teaching Apollo to play the Pan-pipe" (together with a companion-picture hanging near it), is said to have formed one of the compartments of the harpsichord belonging to that great painter. This is the natural magnificence of genius, which thinks no ornaments too precious for the objects of its love. We should like to be rich enough to play at imitating these great men, and see how much we could do to aggrandize a piano-forte. Let us see: it should be of the most precious, aromatic wood; the white keys, ivory (nothing can be better than that); the black, ebony; the legs sculptured with foliage and Loves and Graces; the pannels should all be Titians and Correggios; the most exquisite verses out of the poets should be carved between them; an arabesque cabinet should stand near it, containing the finest compositions; and Rossini should come from Italy to play them, and Pasta to sing.

Meantime, what signifies all this luxury? The soul of music is at hand, wherever there are keys and strings and loving fingers to touch them; and this soul, which disposes us to fancy the luxury, enables us to do without it. We can enjoy it in vision, without the expense.

We take the liberty of closing this article with two copies of verses, which two eminent living musicians, Messrs. Barnett and Novello, have done us the honor to set to music. The verses have been printed before; but many of our readers will not have seen them. We did not think it possible for any words of our own to give us so much pleasure in the repetition, as when we heard her father's composition sung by the pure and most tuneful voice of Miss Clara Novello (Clara is she well named): and the reader may see what is thought of Mr. Barnett's powers, by musical judges, in a criticism upon it in a late number of the "Atlas," or another in a new cheap periodical publication called the "Englishwoman," heiress to the graces and good stock of her deceased parents, the "Ladies' Gazette" and the "Penny Novelist," and uniting them both to better advantage.

THOUGHTS ON HEARING SOME BEAUTIFUL MUSIC.

(*Set to music by Vincent Novello.*)

When lovely sounds about my ears
  Like winds in Eden's tree-tops rise,
And make me, though my spirit hears,
  For very luxury close my eyes;
Let none but friends be round about,
  Who love the smoothing joy like me,
That so the charm be felt throughout,
    And all be harmony.

And when we reach the close divine,
  Then let the hand of her I love
Come with its gentle palm on mine,
  As soft as snow, or lighting dove;
And let, by stealth, that more than friend
  Look sweetness in my opening eyes:
For only so such dreams should end,
    Or wake in Paradise.

THE LOVER OF MUSIC TO HIS PIANO-FORTE.

(*From Barnett's "Lyrical Illustrations of the Modern Poets."*)

O friend, whom glad or grave we seek,
  Heaven-holding shrine!
I ope thee, touch thee, hear thee speak,
  And peace is mine.
No fairy casket, full of bliss,
  Outvalues thee:
Love only, wakened with a kiss,
  More sweet may be.

To thee, when our full hearts o'erflow
  In griefs or joys,
Unspeakable emotions owe
  A fitting voice:
Mirth flies to thee, and Love's unrest,
  And Memory dear;
And Sorrow, with his tightened breast,
  Comes for a tear.

Oh! since no joy of human mould
  Thus waits us still,
Thrice blest be thine, thou gentle fold
  Of peace at will!
No change, no sullenness, no cheat,
  In thee we find:
Thy saddest voice is ever sweet;
  Thine answer, kind.

WHY SWEET MUSIC PRODUCES SADNESS.

SWEET music, that is to say, "sweet" in the sense in which it is evidently used in the following passage, — something not of a mirthful character, but yet not of a melancholy one, — does not always produce sadness; but it does often, even when the words, if it be vocal music, are cheerful. We do not presume to take for granted, that the reason we are about to differ with, or perhaps rather to extend, is Shakespeare's own, or that he would have stopped thus short if speaking in his own person; though he has given it the air of an abstract remark: but Lorenzo, in the "Merchant of Venice," says that it is because our "spirits are attentive."

> "I'm never merry when I hear sweet music,"

says pretty Jessica.

> "The reason is, your spirits are attentive,"

says her lover: —

> "For do but note a wild and wanton herd,
> Or race of youthful and unhandled colts,
> Fetching mad bounds, bellowing and neighing loud,
> Which is the hot condition of their blood;

If they but hear perchance a trumpet sound,
Or any air of music touch their ears,
You shall perceive them make a mutual stand,
Their savage eyes turned to a modest gaze,
By the sweet power of music."

How beautiful! But, with the leave of this young and most elegant logician, his reason is, at least, not sufficient; for how does it account for our being moved, even to tears, by music which is not otherwise melancholy? All attention, it is true, implies a certain degree of earnestness, and all earnestness has a mixture of seriousness: yet seriousness is not the prevailing character of attention in all instances; for we are attentive to fine music, whatever its character; and sometimes it makes us cheerful, and even mirthful. The giddier portions of Rossini's music do not make us sad; Figaro does not make us sad; nor is sadness the general consequence of hearing dances, or even marches.

And yet, again, on the other hand, in the midst of any of this music, even of the most light and joyous, our eye shall sometimes fill with tears. How is this?

The reason surely is, that we have an instinctive sense of the fugitive and perishing nature of all sweet things,—of beauty, of youth, of life; of all those fair shows of the world, of which music seems to be the voice, and of whose transitory nature it reminds us most when it is most beautiful, because it is then that we most regret our mortality.

We do not, it is true, *say* this to ourselves. We are not conscious of the reason; that is to say, we do not feel it with *knowingness:* but we *do* feel it; for the tears are moved. And how many exquisite criticisms of tears and laughter do not whole audiences make at plays, though not one man in fifty shall be able to put down his reasons for it on paper!

DANCING AND DANCERS.

WHILE Tory genius boasts of its poetic Wilson, and ornithology of another, and the fine arts of Wilson, "the English Claude," the minor graces insist upon having their Wilson, too, in the person of the eminent Mr. Thomas Wilson, author of several dramatic pieces, and inductor of ladies and gentlemen into the shapely and salutary art of dancing.

This old, though doubtless, at the same time, ever-young, acquaintance of ours, who has done us the honor for several years past of making us acquainted with his movements, and inviting us to his balls, which it has not been our good fortune to be able to attend, always sends us with his invitations a placard of equal wit and dimensions, in which he takes patriotic occasion to set forth the virtues of his art. He does not affect to despise its ordinary profits, income-wards. That would be a want of candor, unbefitting the entireness of his wisdom. On the contrary, dancing being a liberal art, he is studious to inculcate an equally liberal acknowledgment on the part of those who are indebted to it. But being a man of a reflective turn of leg, and great animal spirits, he omits no opportunity of showing how good his art is for the happiness as well as the graces of his countrymen, — how it renders them light of spirit as well as body, shakes melancholy out of their livers, and will not at all suffer them to be gouty. Nay, he says it is their own fault if they grow old.

We hardly dare to introduce abruptly the remarks on this head, which form the commencement of his present year's *exposé*. But the energy of Mr. Wilson's philanthropy forces its way through his elegances; the good to be done is a greater thing in his mind even than the graces with which he invests it; and in answer to his question, "Why don't everybody dance?" he says, in a passion of sincerity which sweeps objection away with it, "Because the English prefer the pleasures of the table, and sedentary amusements, with their gout, apoplexy, shortness of breath, spindle-shanks, and rum-puncheon bellies," (pardon us, O Bacchus of Anacreon!) "to the more wholesome and healthy recreation of dancing. If you ask a person of fifty" (says he) "to take a dance, the usual reply is, 'My dancing-days are gone by; it's not fit amusement for people of my time of life;' and such like idle cant: for idle cant it really is, as these pretences are either made as excuses for idleness, or to comply with the usual fastidious customs of the day. They manage things better in France, as Yorick says; for it would be quite as difficult amongst that polite and social people to find a person of fifty who did not dance, as it is in gloomy, cold, calculating Old England, to find one who has good sense enough to laugh at these fastidious notions, with a sufficient stock of social animal spirits to share in this polite and exhilarating amusement. Moreover, if we wanted a sanction to continue to dance as long as we are able, I could here give a list (had I room) of a hundred eminent persons who did not consider it a disgrace to dance, even at a very advanced age: amongst the number, Socrates, one of the wisest men and greatest philosophers that ever lived, used to dance for his exercise and amusement when he was upwards of seventy. Read this, ye gourmands and card-players of fifty! and if you are wise, and would leave the gout and a thousand other ills beside you, come *and sport a toe* with me, at 18, Kirby Street, Hatton Garden:—

'For you'll meet many there who to doctors ne'er go;
Who enjoy health and spirit from sporting a toe;
Who neither want powder, pill, mixture, nor lotion,
But a partner and fiddle to set them in motion.'"

Truly we fear that the tip-end of Mr. Wilson's indignant bow strikes hard upon many a venerable gout; and that these dancing philosophers of Kirby Street have the advantage of a great many otherwise sage people, who take pills instead of exercise, and think to substitute powders and lotions for those more ancient usages, yclept the laws of the universe. Such, as Mr. Wilson tells us, was the philosophy of Socrates. There can be no doubt of it: it was the philosophy of all his countrymen, the Greeks, with whom dancing formed a part of their very worship; and who had figures, accordingly, fit to go to church and thank Heaven with. Bacchus himself, with them, was a dancer, and a slender-waisted young gentleman. Such was also the philosophy of Mr. Wilson's brother-poet,

Soame Jenyns, a lively old gentleman of the last century, who wrote a poem on the "Art of Dancing," from which Mr. Wilson should give us some extracts in his next placard (we wish we had it by us); and what is curious, and shows how accustomed these saltatory sages are to consider the interests of the whole human being, spiritual as well as bodily, Mr. Jenyns had a poetical precursor on that subject, who was no less a personage than a chief-justice in the time of Elizabeth, — Sir John Davies; and who, like himself, wrote also on religious matters, and the "Immortality of the Soul." Sir John, however, appears not to have sufficiently practised his own precepts; for he died of apoplexy at fifty-seven, — a very crude and juvenile age, according to Mr. Wilson. But then he was a lawyer, and injudicious enough to be a judge, — to sit bundled up in cloth and ermine, instead of dancing in a "light simar." Again: there was Sir Christopher Hatton, chancellor in the time of Elizabeth, who is said to have absolutely danced himself into that venerable position through a series of extraordinary steps of court favor, commencing in a ballroom, and not improbably either; for, like some of his great brethren in that office, Sir Christopher appears to have been a truly universal genius; able, "like the elephant's trunk," to pick up his pin as well as knock down his tiger; and it is not to be wondered at if sovereigns sometimes get at a knowledge of the profounder faculties of a man through the medium of his more entertaining ones. The chancellor, however, appears to have turned his dancing to no better account, ultimately, than the justice; for they say he died prematurely of a broken heart, because the queen pressed him for a debt, — an end worthier of a courtier than of a sage and dancer. This it is to acquire legal habits, and "make the worse appear the better reason," even to one's self. Hatton should have been above his law, and stuck to his legs, — to his natural *understanding*, as Mr. Wilson would call it; and then nothing would have overthrown him. Gray, with a poet's license, represents him as dancing after he was chancellor. It is a pity it was not true.

> "My grave lord-keeper led the brawls:
> His seal and maces danced before him.
> His high-crowned hat and satin doublet
> Moved the stout heart of England's queen,
> Though pope and Spaniard could not trouble it."

Sir Christopher bequeathed his name to Hatton Garden; so that Mr. Wilson resides in a fit neighborhood, and doubtless has visions of cavaliers, and maids of honor, in ruffs, "sporting their toes" through his dreams by night.

Our artist's vindication of the juvenility of dancers at fifty reminds us of a pleasant realization we experienced the other day of a stage joke; nay, of a great improvement on it, — a romance of real life! In one of Colman's farces, an old man, hearing another called old, and understanding he was only forty, exclaims, "Forty! — quite a boy!" We heard this opinion pronounced upon a man of *sixty* by an old gentleman, who, we suppose, must be eighty, or thereabouts. It was in an omnibus, in which he was returning from a city dinner, jovial and toothless, his rosy gills gracing his white locks; an Anacreon in broadcloth. Some friend of his was telling him of the death of an acquaintance, and, in answer to his question respecting the cause of it, said he did not know, but that the deceased was "sixty years of age." The remark seemed hardly to be an indiscretion in the ears of the venerable old boy, he considered it so very inapplicable. "Sixty!" cried he, with a lisp that was really robust: "well, that's nothing, you know, compared with *life!* Why, he was quite a boy!"

Wilson. This must have been a dancer.

Seer. Or a rider.

W. Well, horseback is a kind of dancing.

Seer. Or a walker.

W. Well, walking is dancing too; that is to say, good walking. You know, my dear sir, people are said to "walk a minuet."

Seer. But they say dancers are not good walkers.

W. How! — dancers not good walkers! It is true, I must allow in candor, that some professional dancers are apt to turn out their toes a little too much; but not all, my dear sir — not the best: and as to dancers in general, I will affirm, *meo periculo*, as the philosopher says, they walk exquisitely, — *à merveille.* Come and see my dancers walking into the ball-room, or my new dance of the "Rival Beauties:" "thirty young ladies," sir, all moving to the sweet and peaceful battle at once. See how *they* walk, my dear sir! You would never forget it.

Seer. I shall never forget it, as it is, Mr. Wilson. I see it, in imagination, painted in the beautiful red letters of your placard; and do not wonder that you are a man in request for Richmond parties, and records of it in verse.

Here Mr. Wilson finishes the dialogue with a bow, to which it would be bad taste and an anti-climax to reply. There is a final and triumphant silence of eloquence, to which nothing can be said.

To return to the matter of age. There can be no doubt that dancers of fifty are a very different sort of quinquegenarians from sitters of fifty, and that men of the same age often resemble each other in no other respect. "The same is not the same." Some people may even be said to have begun life over again at a time when the dissipated and the sullen are preparing to give it up. It is not necessary to mention such cases as those of Old Parr. Marmontel—a man of letters, of taste and fancy, and therefore, it is to be presumed, of no very coarse organization—married at fifty-six; and, after living happily with a family born to him, died at the age of seventy-seven. But though a man of letters, and living at a period when there was great license of manners, to which his own had formed no very rigid exception, he had led, upon the whole, a natural life, and was temperate. Besides, Nature is very indulgent to those who do not violently contradict her with artificial habits, excesses of the table, or sullen thoughts. She hates alike the extremes, not of cheerfulness, but of Comus and of Melancholy. A venerable peer of Norfolk, now living, married, and had an heir born to his estate, at a venerable age, which nobody thought of treating with jests of a certain kind; for he also had been a denizen of the natural world, and was as young, with good sense and exercise, as people of half his age, — far younger than many. We remember the face of envying respect and astonishment with which the news was received by "a person of wit and honor about town" (now deceased), in whose company we happened to be at the moment, and who might have been his son three or four times over.

Query, at what age must a person take to venerable manners, and consent to look old if he does not feel so? Mr. Wilson will say, "When he is forced to leave off dancing." And there is a definite notion in that. If any one, therefore, wishes to have precise ideas on this point, and behave himself as becomes his real, not his chronological, time of life, we really think he cannot do better than study in Kirby Street, or at Willis's, and learn to know at what age it becomes him to be reverend, or how long he may continue laughing at those who remonstrate with him because they hobble. Linnæus in his "Travels" gives an account — ludicrous in the eyes of us spectators of the staid and misgiving manners of people at the same time of life — of two Laplanders who accompanied him on some occasion, — we forget what, — but who carried bundles for him, and had otherwise reason for being tired, the way being long. One of them was fifty, the other considerably older; yet what did these old boys at the close of their journey, but, instead of sitting down and resting themselves, begin laughing and running about *after one another*, like a couple of antediluvian children, as if they had just risen! They wanted nothing but pinafores, and a mother remonstrating with them for not coming and having their hairs combed.

Most people are astonished, perhaps, as they advance beyond the period of youth and middle life, at not finding themselves still older; and, if they took wise advantage of this astonishment, they would all live to a much greater age. It is equally by not daring to be too young, nor consenting to be too old, that men keep themselves in order with Nature, and in heart with her. We kill ourselves before our time with artificial irregularities and melancholy resentments. We hasten age with late hours, and the table, and want of exercise; and hate it, and make it worse when it comes, with bad temper and inactive regrets.

A boy of ten thinks he shall be in the prime of life when he is twenty, and (as lives go) he is so; though, when he comes to be twenty, he shoves off his notion of the prime to thirty, then to thirty-five, then to forty; and when, at length, he is forced to own himself no longer young, he is at once astonished to think he has been young so long, and angry to find himself no younger. This would be hardly fair upon the indulgence of Nature, if Nature supplied us with education as well as existence, and the world itself did not manifestly take time to come to years of discretion. In the early ages of the world, the inability to lead artificial lives was the great cause of longevity; as in future ones, it is to be hoped, the appreciation of the natural life will bring men round to it. It would have put the pastoral, patriarchal people sadly out, to keep late hours at night, and to sit after dinner "pushing about" the *milk!*

Nature, in the mean time, acts with her usual good-natured instinct, and makes the best of a bad business; rather, let us say, produces it in order to produce a better, and to enable us to improve upon her early world. She has even something good to say in behalf of the ill-health of modern times and the rich delicacy of its perceptions: so that we might be warranted in supposing that she is ever improving, even when she least appears to be so; and that your pastoral longevity, though a good pattern in some respects for that which is to come, had but a poor milk-and-water measure of happiness, compared with the wine and the intellectual movement of us intermediate strugglers. At all events, the measure, somehow or other, may be equal, and the difference only a variety of sameness. And there is as much comfort in that reflection, and a great difficulty solved in it. Only Nature, after all, still incites us to look forward; and, whether it be for the sake of real or of apparent change, forward we must look, and look heartily, taking care to realize all the happiness we can as we go. This seems the true mode of keeping all our faculties in action, — all the inevitable thoughts given to man, of past, present, and future; and, with this grave reflection, we conclude our present dance under Mr. Wilson's patronage, gravely as well as gayly recommending his very useful art to all lovers of health, grace, and sociality.

Why do not people oftener get up dances at home, and without waiting for the ceremony of visitors and the drawback of late hours? It would be a great addition to the cheerfulness and health of families.

TWELFTH NIGHT.

A Street Portrait.—Shakespeare's Play.—Recollections of a Twelfth Night.

CHRISTMAS goes out in fine style,—with Twelfth Night. It is a finish worthy of the time. Christmas Day was the morning of the season; New Year's Day the middle of it, or noon; Twelfth Night is the night, brilliant with innumerable planets of Twelfth-cakes. The whole island keeps court; nay, all Christendom. All the world are kings and queens. Everybody is somebody else, and learns at once to laugh at, and to tolerate, characters different from his own, by enacting them. Cakes, characters, forfeits, lights, theatres, merry rooms, little holiday-faces, and last, not least, the painted sugar on the cakes, so bad to eat, but so fine to look at, useful because it is perfectly useless except for a sight and a moral,—all conspire to throw a giddy splendor over the last night of the season, and to send it to bed in pomp and colors like a prince.

And not the least good thing in Twelfth Night is, that we see it coming for days beforehand in the cakes that garnish the shops. We are among those who do not "like a surprise," except in dramas (and not too much of it even there, nor unprepared with expectation). We like to know of the good things intended for us. It adds the pleasure of hope to that of possession. Thus we eat our Twelfth-cake many times in imagination before it comes. Every pastry-cook's shop we pass flashes it upon us.

> "Coming *Twelfth-cakes* cast their shadows before;"

if shadows they can be called, which shade have none; so full of color are they, as if Titian had invented them. Even the little ragged boys, who stand at those shops by the hour, admiring the heaven within, and are destined to have none of it, get, perhaps from imagination alone, a stronger taste of the beatitude than many a richly fed palate which is at the mercy of some particular missing relish, — some touch of spice or citron, or a "leetle more" egg.

We believe we have told a story of one of those urchins before; but it will bear repetition, especially as a strong relish of it has come upon us, and we are tempted to relate it at greater length. There is nothing very wonderful or epigrammatic in it; but it has to do with the beatific visions of the pastry-shops. Our hero was one of those equivocal animal-spirits of the streets, who come whistling along, you know not whether thief or errand-boy, sometimes with bundle and sometimes not, in corduroys, a jacket, and a cap, or bit of hat, with hair sticking through a hole in it. His vivacity gets him into scrapes in the street, and he is not ultra-studious of civility in his answers. If the man he runs against is not very big, he gives him abuse for abuse at once; if otherwise, he gets at a convenient distance, and then halloos out, "Eh, stupid!" or, "Can't you see before you?" or, "Go, and get your face washed!" This last is a favorite saying of his, out of an instinct referable to his own visage. He sings "Hokee-pokee" and a "Shiny Night," varied occasionally with an uproarious "Rise, gentle Moon!" or, "Coming through the Rye." On winter evenings, you may hear him indulging himself, as he goes along, in a singular undulation of howl, — a sort of gargle, — as if a wolf were practising the rudiments of a shake. This he delights to do more particularly in a crowded thoroughfare, as though determined that his noise should triumph over every other, and show how jolly he is, and how independent of the ties to good behavior. If the street is a quiet one, and he has a stick in his hand (perhaps a hoop-stick), he accompanies the howl with a run upon the gamut of the iron rails. He is the nightingale of mud and cold. If he gets on in life, he will be a pot-boy. At present, as we said before, we hardly know what he is; but his mother thinks herself lucky if he is not transported.

Well, one of these elves of the *pavé* — perplexers of lord-mayors, and irritators of the police — was standing one evening before a pastry-cook's shop-window, flattening his nose against the glass, and watching the movements of a school-boy who was in the happy agony of selecting the best bunn. He had stood there ten minutes before the boy came in, and had made himself acquainted with all the eatables lying before him, and wondered at the slowness and apparent indifference of jaws masticating tarts. His interest, great before, is now intense. He follows the new-comer's eye and hand, hither and thither. His own arm feels like the other's arm. He shifts the expression of his mouth and the shrug of his body at every perilous approximation which the chooser makes to a second-rate bunn. He is like a bowler following the nice inflections of the bias; for he wishes him nothing but success: the occasion is too great for envy. He feels all the generous smypathy of a knight of old, when he saw another within an ace of winning some glorious prize, and his arm doubtful of the blow.

At length, the awful decision is made, and the bunn laid hands on.

"*Yah!* you fool!" exclaims the watcher, bursting with all the despair and indignation of knowing boyhood, "you have *left the biggest!*"

Twelfth-cake and its king and queen are in honor of the crowned-heads who are said to have brought presents to Jesus in his cradle, — a piece of royal service not necessary to be believed in by good Christians, though very proper to be maintained among the gratuitous decorations with which good and poetical hearts willingly garnish their faith. "The Magi, or Wise Men, are vulgarly called (says a note in 'Brand's Popular Antiquities,' quarto edition by Ellis, p. 19) the three kings of Collen (Cologne). The first, named Melchior, an aged man with a long beard, offered gold; the second, Jasper, a beardless youth, offered frankincense; the third, Balthaser, a black, or Moor, with a large spreading beard, offered myrrh." This picture is full of color, and has often been painted. The word Epiphany (Επιφανεια, *superapparitio*, an appearance from above) alludes to the star which is described in the Bible as guiding the wise men. In Italy, the word has been corrupted into Beffania, or Beffana (as in England it used to be called Piffany); and Beffana, in some parts of that country, has come to mean an old fairy, or Mother Bunch, whose figure is carried about the streets, and who rewards or punishes children at night by putting sweetmeats, or stones and dirt, into a stocking hung up for the purpose near the bed's head. The word *Beffa*, taken from this, familiarly means a trick or mockery put upon any one: to such base uses may come the most splendid terms! Twelfth Day, like the other old festivals of the Church of old, has had a link of connection found for it with Pagan customs, and has been traced to the Saturnalia of the ancients, when people drew lots for imaginary kingdoms. Its observation is still kept up with more or less ceremony all over Christendom. In Paris, they enjoy it with their usual vivacity. The king there is chosen, not by drawing a paper as with us, but by the lot of a bean which falls to him, and which is put into the cake; and great ceremony is observed when the king or the queen "drink:" which once gave rise to a jest, that occasioned the damnation of a play of Voltaire's. The play was performed at this season; and, a queen in it having to die by poison, a wag exclaimed with Twelfth-Night solemnity, when her majesty was about to take it, "The queen drinks!" The joke was infectious, and the play died as well as the poor queen.

Many a pleasant Twelfth Night have we passed in our time: and such future Twelfth Nights as may remain to us shall be pleasant, God and good-will permitting; for, even if care should be round about them, we have no notion of missing these mountain-tops of rest and brightness, on which people may refresh themselves during the stormiest parts of life's voyage. Most assuredly will we look forward to them, and stop there when we arrive, as though we had not to begin buffeting again the next day. No joy or consolation that heaven or earth affords us will we ungratefully pass by; but prove, by our acceptance and relish of it, that it is what it is said to be, and that we deserve to have it. "The child is father to the man;" and a very foolish-grown boy he is, and unworthy of his sire, if he is not man enough to know when to be like him. What! shall he go and sulk in a corner, because life is not just what he would have it? Or shall he discover that his dignity will not bear the shaking of holiday merriment, being too fragile, and likely to tumble to pieces? Or, lastly, shall he take himself for too good and perfect a person to come within the chance of contamination from a little ultra life and wassail-bowl, and render it necessary to have the famous question thrown at his stately and stupid head, —

"Dost thou think, because thou art virtuous, there shall be no more cakes and ale?"

This passage is in "Twelfth Night," the last play (be it never forgotten) * which Shakespeare is understood to have written, and which shows how, in his beautiful and universal mind, the belief in love, friend-

* This opinion of Malone's has been ably set aside by Mr. Knight. The spirit of the Shakespearian wisdom still, however, remains.

ship and joy, and all good things, survived his knowledge of all evil, — affording us an everlasting argument against the conclusions of minor men of the world, and enabling the meanest of us to dare to avow the same faith.

Here is another lecture to false and unseasonable notions of gravity, in the same play: —

"I protest (quoth the affected steward Malvolio), I take these wise men, that crow so at these set kind of fools, to be no better than the fools' zanies.

"Oh! (says the Lady Olivia,) you are sick of self-love, Malvolio, and taste with a distempered appetite. To be generous, guiltless, and of free disposition, is to take those things for bird-bolts, that you deem cannon-bullets."

This is the play in which are those beautiful passages about music, love, friendship, &c., which have as much of the morning of life in them as any that the great poet ever wrote, and are painted with as rosy and wet a pencil: —

"If music be the food of love," &c.

"Away before me to sweet beds of flowers:
Love-thoughts lie rich when canopied with bowers."

"She never told her love,
But let concealment, like a worm i' the bud,
Feed on her damask cheek," &c.

"I hate ingratitude more in a man,"

says the refined and exquisite Viola,

"Than lying, vainness, babbling, drunkenness,
Or any taint of vice, whose strong corruption
Inhabits our frail blood."

And again: —

"In Nature there's no blemish, but the mind:"

[that is to say, the faults of the mind:]

"*None can be called deformed but the unkind.*"

The play of "Twelfth Night," with proper good taste, is generally performed, at the theatres, *on* Twelfth Night. There is little or nothing belonging to the occasion in it, except a set of merry-makers who carouse all night, and sing songs enough to "draw three souls out of one weaver." It is evident that Shakespeare was at a loss for a title to his play; for he has called it "Twelfth Night, or *What You Will:*" but the nocturnal revels reminded him of the anniversary, which, being the player and humorist that he was, and accustomed, doubtless, to many a good sitting-up, appears to have stood forth prominently among his recollections of the year. So that it is probable he kept up his Twelfth Night to the last: assuredly he kept up his merry and romantic characters, his Sir Tobies and his Violas. And, keeping up his stage faith *so well*, he must needs have kept up his home faith. He could not have done it otherwise. He would invite his Stratford friends to "king and queen;" and, however he might have looked in face, would still have felt young in heart towards the budding daughters of his visitors, the possible Violas perhaps of some love-story of their own, and not more innocent in "the last recesses of the mind" than himself.

We spent a Twelfth Night once, which, by common consent of the parties concerned, was afterwards known by the name of *the* Twelfth Night. It was doubted among us, not merely whether ourselves, but whether anybody else, ever *had* such a Twelfth Night: —

> "For never, since created *cake*,
> Met such untiring force, as, named with these,
> Could merit more than that small infantry
> Which *goes to bed betimes*."

The evening began with such tea as is worth mention; for we never knew anybody make it like the maker. Dr. Johnson would have given it his placidest growl of approbation. Then, with piano-forte, violin, and violoncello, came Handel, Corelli, and Mozart. Then followed the drawing for king and queen, in order that the "small infantry" might have their due share of the night, without sitting up *too* too late (for a reasonable "too-late" is to be allowed once and away). Then games of all the received kinds, forgetting no branch of Christmas customs. And very good extempore blank verse was spoken by some of the court (for our characters imitated a court), not unworthy of the wit and dignity of Tom Thumb. Then came supper, and all characters were soon forgotten but the feasters' own: good and lively souls, and festive all, both male and female, — with a constellation of the brightest eyes that we had ever seen met together. This fact was so striking, that a burst of delighted assent broke forth, when Moore's charming verses were struck up; —

> "To ladies' eyes a round, boys,
> We can't refuse, we can't refuse;
> For bright eyes so abound, boys,
> 'Tis hard to choose, 'tis hard to choose."

The bright eyes, the beauty, the good humor, the wine, the wit, the poetry (for we had celebrated wits and poets among us, as well as charming women), fused all hearts together in one unceasing round of fancy and laughter, till *breakfast;* to which we adjourned in a room full of books, the authors of which might almost have been waked up and embodied to come among us. Here, with the bright eyes literally as bright as ever at six o'clock in the morning (we all remarked it), we merged one glorious day into another, as a good omen (for it was also fine weather, though in January); and, as luck and our good faith would have it, the door was no sooner opened to let forth the ever-joyous visitors, than the trumpets of a regiment quartered in the neighborhood struck up into the morning air, seeming to blow forth triumphant approbation, and as if they sounded purely to do us honor, and to say, "You are as early and untired as we."

We do not recommend such nights to be "resolved on," much less to be made a system of regular occurrence. They should flow out of the impulse, as this did; for there was no intention of sitting up so late. But so genuine was that night, and so true a recollection of pleasure did it leave upon the minds of all who shared it, that it has helped to stamp a seal of selectness upon the house in which it was passed, and which, for the encouragement of good-fellowship and of humble aspirations towards *tree-planting*, we are here incited to point out: for, by the same token, the writer of these papers planted some plane-trees within the rails by the garden-gate (selecting the plane in honor of the Genius of Domesticity, to which it was sacred among the Greeks) ; and anybody who does not disdain to look at a modest tenement for the sake of the happy hours that have been spent in it, may know it by those trees, as he passes along the row of houses called York Buildings, in the New Road, Marylebone. A man may pique himself without vanity upon having planted a tree; and, humble as our performance has been that way, we confess we are glad of it, and have often looked at the result with pleasure. The reader would smile, perhaps sigh (but a pleasure would or should be at the bottom of his sigh), if he knew what consolation we had experienced in some very trying seasons, merely from seeing those trees growing up, and affording shade and shelter to passengers, as well as a bit of leafiness to the possessor of the house. *Every one should plant a tree who can.** It is one of the cheapest, as well as easiest, of all tasks; and, if a man cannot reckon upon enjoying the shade much himself (which is the reason why trees are not planted everywhere), it is surely worth while to bequeathe so pleasant and useful a memorial of himself to others. They are green footsteps of our existence, which show that we have not lived in vain.

"Dig a well, plant a tree, write a book, and go to heaven," says the Arabian proverb. We cannot exactly dig a well. The parish authorities would not employ us. Besides, wells are not so much wanted in England as in Arabia, nor books either; otherwise we should be two-thirds on our road to heaven already.

* Young trees from nursery-grounds are very cheap, and cost less than flowers.

But trees are wanted, and ought to be wished for, almost everywhere, especially amidst the hard brick and mortar of towns; so that we may claim at least one-third of the way, having planted more than one tree in our time: and, if our books cannot wing our flight much higher (for they never pretended to be any thing greater than birds singing among the trees), we have other merits, thank Heaven! than our own to go upon; and shall endeavor to piece out our frail and most imperfect ladder with all the good things we can love and admire in God's creation.

RULES IN MAKING PRESENTS.

F the present is to be very exquisite indeed, and no mortification will be mixed up with the receipt of it, out of pure inability to make an equal one, or from any other cause, the rule has often been laid down. It should be something useful, beautiful, costly, and rare. It is generally an elegance, however, to omit the costliness. The rarity is the great point; because riches themselves cannot always command it, and the peculiarity of the compliment is the greater. Rare present to rare person.

If you are rich, it is a good rule in general to make a rich present; that is to say, one equal, or at least not dishonorable, to your means: otherwise you set your riches above your friendship and generosity; which is a mean mistake.

Among equals, it is a good rule not to exceed the equality of resources; otherwise there is a chance of giving greater mortification than pleasure, unless to a mean mind; and it does not become a generous one to care for having advantages over a mind like that.

But a rich man may make a present far richer than can be made him in return, provided the receiver be as generous and understanding as he, and knows that there will be no mistake on either side. In this case, an opportunity of giving himself great delight is afforded to the rich man; and he can only have or bestow it under those circumstances.

On the other hand, a poor man, if he is generous, and understood to be so, may make the very poorest of presents, and give it an exquisite value; for his heart and his understanding will accompany it; and the very daring to send his straw will show that he has a spirit above his means, and such as could bestow and enrich the costliest present. But the certainty of his being thus generous, and having this spirit, must be very great. It would be the miserablest and most despicable of all mistakes, and in all probability the most self-betraying too, to send a poor present under a shabby pretence.

With no sort of presents must there be pretence. People must not say (and say falsely) that they could get no other, or that they could afford no better; nor must they affect to think better of the present than it is worth; nor, above all, keep asking about it after it is given, — how you like it, whether you find it useful, &c.

It is often better to give no present at all than one beneath your means, — always, should there be a misgiving on the side of the bestower.

One present in the course of a life is generosity from some: from others, it is but a sacrifice made to avoid giving more.

To receive a present handsomely and in a right spirit, even when you have none to give in return, is to give one in return.

We must not send presents to strangers (except of a very common and trifling nature, and not without some sort of warrant even then), unless we are sure of our own right and good motives in sending it, and of the right and inclination, too, which they would have to permit themselves to receive it: otherwise we pay both parties a very ill compliment, and such as no modest and honorable spirit on either side would venture upon. There might, it is true, be a state of society in which such ventures would not be quite so hardy; and it is possible, meanwhile, that a very young and enthusiastic nature, in its ignorance of the perplexities that at present beset the world, might here and there hazard it: but probably a good deal of self-love would be mixed up with the proceeding. The only possible exception would be in the case of a great and rare genius, which had a right to make laws to itself, and to suppose that its notice was acquaintanceship sufficient.

ROMANCE OF COMMONPLACE.

EVERY sentiment, or want of sentiment, pushed to excess, bears, from that excess, a character of romance: even dulness may be romantic. We remember our late dear friend Charles Lamb, many years ago, giving us, with his exquisite tact, an account of a deceased acquaintance of his who carried "commonplace" itself to a pitch of the "romantic," and who would waylay you for half an hour with a history of his having cut his finger or mislaid a pair of shoes. This gentleman did not draw infinite somethings out of nothing, like the wits of the "Lutrin" or the "Rape of the Lock," or the Italian expatiators upon a cough or a Christian name. He got hold of nothing, and out of it, with a congeniality of emptiness, drew nothing whatever. But it was *he* that drew the nothing, and *you* that listened to him; and thus he got a sense of himself somehow. If you ran against him in the street, it was an event in his life, and enabled him to stand breathing and smiling, and saying how much it did *not* signify, for the next intense five minutes. He once met a lady, an acquaintance of his, who was going to have a tooth drawn.

"Dear me, madam! and so you are going to have your tooth drawn?"

"Yes, sir."

"By Mr. Parkinson, I presume?"

"Yes."

"Dear me! I fear you have suffered a good deal, madam?"

"Not a little, indeed."

"God bless me! I am very sorry to hear it, — *very* sorry. How long, pray, may you have suffered this toothache?"

"I should think, a week."

"God bless me! A week! That is a long time! And by night as well as by day, I presume?"

"I have hardly had any sleep these two nights."

"Dear me! That is very sad. God bless me! No sleep for these two nights! Want of sleep is a very sad thing, — highly distressing. I could not do without my regular sleep. No, no: none of us can. It is highly undermining to the constitution; produces such fatigue, such lassitude, such weariness! *H'm! h'm!*" (*Humming with a sort of sympathy and gentlemanly groan, as if his own face were bound up.*) "I see you are suffering now, madam?"

"It will be soon over now."

"*H'm!* You are very bold, madam, — very resolute; but that is extremely sensible. *H'm!* Dear me! And you have tried clove, I presume, and all that?"

"Why, I am not young, and do not like to part with my teeth."

"Ah — oh — *h'm!* just so — very natural — ah — yes — dear me! *h'm!* A double tooth, I suppose?"

(*The lady nods.*)

"Ah — afraid of the cold air — you are right not to open your mouth, madam. Cold gets in. Ah — *h'm* — yes, just so." (*Nodding, bowing, and groaning.*)

(*Lady turns to go up a court, and makes a gesture of bidding him good-morning.*)

"Oh — ah — dear me! ay, this is the place — so it is — I wish you a happy release, madam — I hope the process will be easy — *h'm!* ha-a-ah!" (*Takes farewell between a sort of breath and a groan. Lady goes into the dentist's, has her tooth drawn, and, on returning down the court, is astonished to find the gentleman waiting at the corner to congratulate her.*)*

"Well, madam" (*bowing and smiling*), "the tooth is drawn, I presume?"

(*Lady acquiesces.*)

"Dear me! ah! — *h'm!* — very painful, I fear — a long while drawing?"

Lady. 'Tis out, at last. (*Aside.* I wonder when the man will have done with his absurdity.)

"A skilful dentist, Mr. Parkinson, madam?"

(*Lady acquiesces.*)

"I have not been to a dentist myself these — let me see — ah, yes, it must be — now these twenty years. I had one bad tooth, and caught a cold sitting in the draught of a coach — very dangerous thing — and chaises are worse — very dangerous things, chaises — *h'm* — very. You are suffering still, I see, madam? from the *ghost* of the tooth, I presume?" (*laughing.*)

* A fact.

"But, dear me! I am keeping you in the draught of this court, and you go the other way. *Good*-morning, madam! Good-morning! I wish you a very GOOD-morning! Don't speak, I beg. GOOD-morning!"

And so, thus heaping emphasis upon emphasis upon this very new valediction, and retaining a double smile amidst his good wishes, from his very new joke about the ghost of a tooth, our hero of Commonplace takes his leave.

AMIABLENESS SUPERIOR TO INTELLECT.

IN our article upon the gossiping old gentleman who appeared to sympathize so excessively with the lady's toothache, we omitted to caution some of our readers against supposing that we were contradicting our usual sympathetic theories, and laughing at any innocent exemplification of them, however trivial. But though the gentleman was harmless, except in his tediousness, and not an ill-natured man, and did far better than if he had set himself to waste an equal portion of time in the manifestation of antipathy, yet sympathy was not the ground of his proceeding: it was pure want of ideas, and a sensation, — the necessity of killing time. We should not object even to any innocent mode of doing that, where a human being lives under a necessity so unfortunate, and has not the luck to be a hedger or ditcher; but it is desirable not to let sympathy be mistaken for something different from what it is, especially where it takes a shape that is ridiculous.

On the other hand, with regard to the commonplace of the matter, apart from an absolute extravagance of insipidity, far are we from wishing to treat commonplaces with derision, purely as such. They are the common clay of which human intercourse is made, and therefore as respectable in our eyes as any other of the ordinary materials of our planet, however desirous we may be of warming them into flowers. Nay, flowers they have, provided the clay be pure and kindly. The air of health and cheerfulness is over them. They are like the common grass, and the daisies and buttercups. Children have them; and what children have, the most uncommon grown people may envy, unless they have health and cheerfulness too.

It is Sir Walter Scott, we believe, who has observed somewhere, that men of superior endowments, or other advantages, are accustomed to pay too little regard to the intercourse of their less-gifted fellow-creatures, and to regret all the time that is passed in their company. He says they accustom themselves so much to the living upon sweets and spices, that they lose a proper relish for ordinary food, and grow contemptuous of those who subsist upon it, to the injury of their own enjoyment. They keep their palate in a constant state of thirst and irritation, rather than of healthy satisfaction. And we recollect Mr. Hazlitt making a remark to a similar effect; namely, that the being accustomed to the society of men of genius renders the conversation of others tiresome, as consisting of a parcel of things that have been heard a thousand times, and from which no stimulus is to be obtained. He lamented this as an effect unbecoming a reflecting man and a fellow-creature (for though irritable, and sometimes resentful, his heart was large, and full of humanity); and the consequence was, that nobody paid greater attention than he to common conversation, or showed greater respect towards any endeavors to interest him, however trite. Youths of his acquaintance are fond of calling to mind the footing of equality on which he treated them, even when children; gravely interchanging remarks with them, as he sat side by side, like one grown person with another, and giving them now and then (though without the pomp) a Johnsonian, "Sir." The serious earnestness of his "Indeed, m'um!" with lifted eyebrows, and protruded lips, while listening to the surprising things told him by good housewives about their shopping or their preserves, is now sounding in our ears; and makes us long to see again the splenetic but kindly philosopher, who worried himself to death about the good of the nations.

There is but one thing necessary to put any reflecting person at his ease with commonplace people; and that is, their own cheerfulness and good-humor. To be able to be displeased, in spite of this, is to be insensible to the best results of wisdom itself. When all the Miss Smiths meet all the Miss Joneses, and there is nothing but a world of smiles and recognitions and gay breath, and loud askings after this person and that, and comparisons of bonnets and cloaks, and "So glads!" and "So sorrys!" and rosy cheeks, or more lovely good-natured lips, who that has any good humor of his own, or power to extract a pleasant thought from pleasant things, desires wit or genius in this full-blown exhibition of comfortable humanity? He might as well be sullen at not finding wit or genius in a cart full of flowers, going along the street, or in the spring cry of "Primroses."

A total want of ideas in a companion, or of the power to receive them, is indeed to be avoided by men who require intellectual excitement; but it is a great mistake to suppose that the most discerning men demand intellect above every thing else in their most habitual associates, much less in general intercourse. Happy would they be to see intellect more universally extended, but as a means, not as an end, — as a help to the knowledge of what is amiable, and not what is merely knowing. Clever men are sometimes said even to be jealous of clever companions, especially female ones. Men of genius, it is notorious, for a very different reason, and out of their own imagination of what is excellent, and their power to adorn what they love, will be enamoured, in their youth, of women neither intelligent nor amiable nor handsome. They make them all three with their fancy; and are sometimes too apt, in after-life, to resent what is nobody's fault but their own. However, their faults have their excuses, as well as those of other men: only they who know most should excuse most. But the reader may take our word for it, from the experience of long intercourse with such men, that what they value above every other consideration in a companion, female or male, is amiableness; that is to say, evenness of temper, and the willingness (general as well as particular) to please and be pleased, without egotism and without exaction. This is what we have ever felt to be the highest thing in themselves, and gave us a preference for them, infinite, above others of their own class of power. We know of nothing capable of standing by the side of it, or of supplying its place, but one; and that is a deep interest in the welfare of mankind. The possession of this may sometimes render the very want of amiableness touching, because it seems to arise from the reverse of what is unamiable and selfish, and to be exasperated, not because itself is unhappy, but because others are so. It was this, far more than his intellectual endowments (great as they were), which made us like Mr. Hazlitt. Many a contest has it saved us with him, many a sharp answer, and interval of alienation; and often, perhaps, did he attribute to an apprehension of his formidable powers (for which, in our animal spirits, we did not care twopence) what was owing entirely to our love of the sweet drop at the bottom of his heart. But only imagine a man who should feel this interest too, and be deeply amiable, and have great sufferings, bodily and mental, and know his own errors, and waive the claims of his own virtues, and manifest an unceasing considerateness for the comfort of those about him, in the very least as well as greatest things; surviving, in the pure life of his heart, all mistake, all misconception, all exasperation, and ever having a soft word in his extremity, not only for those who consoled, but for those who distressed him; and imagine how we must have loved *him!* It was Mr. Shelley. His genius, transcendent as it was, would not have bound us to him; his poetry, his tragedy, his philosophy, would not have bound us; no, not even his generosity, had it been less amiable. It was his unbounded heart and his ever-kind speech. Now, observe, pray, dear reader, that what was most delightful in such a man as this, is most delightful, in its degree, in all others; and that people are loved, not in proportion to their intellect, but in proportion to their lovability. Intellectual powers are the leaders of the world, but only for the purpose of guiding them into the promised land of peace and amiableness or of showing them encouraging pictures of it by the way. They are no more the things to live with or repose with, apart from qualities of the heart and temper, than the means are without the end; or than a guide to a pleasant spot is the spot itself, with its trees, health, and quiet.

It has been truly said, that knowledge is of the head, but wisdom is of the heart; that is, you may know a great many things, but turn them to no good account of life and intercourse, without a certain harmony of nature often possessed by those whose knowledge is little or nothing. Many a man is to be found, who knows what amiableness is, without being amiable; and many an amiable man, who would be put to the blush if you expected of him a knowing definition of amiableness. But there are a great many people held to be very knowing, and entertaining the opinion themselves, who, in fact, are only led by that opinion to think they may dispense with being amiable, and who, in so thinking, confute their pretension to knowingness. The truth is, that knowledge is by no means so common a thing as people suppose it; while luckily, on the other hand, wisdom is much less uncommon: for it has been held a proof of one of the greatest instances of knowledge that ever existed, that it knew how little it *did* know! whereas everybody is wise in proportion as he is happy or patient; that is to say, in proportion as he makes the best of good or bad fortune.

LIFE AFTER DEATH.—BELIEF IN SPIRITS.

WE made use of an inaccurate expression in a communication to a correspondent the other day, which we take the liberty of thus publicly correcting. We spoke of man as a "finite" creature. The term, strictly speaking, does not convey the meaning we intended. *Finis* is an end; and finite might imply a being whose end, or utter termination, was known and certain. Assuredly we wrote the word in no such spirit of presumption. All our writings will testify, that we are of a religion which enjoys the most unbounded hopes of man, both here and hereafter. By finite, we meant to imply a creature of limited powers and circumscribed *present* existence. Far were we from daring to lift up mortal finger against immortal futurity. Religion itself must first be put out of man's heart, and the very stars out of the sky, and no such words be remembered as sentiment and imagination and memory, and hope too, ay, and reason, before we should presume to say what end ought to be put to these endless aspirations of the soul.

We are for making the most of the present world, as if there were no hereafter; and the most of hereafter, as if there were no present world. We think that God and Christianity and utility and imagination and right reason, and whatsoever is complete and harmonious in the constitution of the human faculties, however opposed it may seem, enjoin us to do BOTH. We are surprised, notwithstanding the allowance to be made for the great diversity of Christian sects, how any Christian, calling himself such by the least right of discipline, can undervalue the utmost human endeavors in behalf of this world, the utmost cultivation of this one (among others) of the manifest and starry gardens of God; but we are most of all surprised at it in those that adhere the most literally to injunction and prophecy, while they know how to confine the fugitive and conventional uses of the terms "this world," &c., &c., to their proper meanings.

In the feasibility of this consummation, the most infidel utilitarian is of the same faith with the most believing Christian, and so far is—

"The best good Christian he,
Although he knows it not."

Now, he is only to carry his beloved reason a little farther, and he will find himself on the confines of the most unbounded hopes of another world, as well as of the present; for reason itself, in its ordinary sense, will tell him that it is reasonable to make the utmost of all his faculties, imagination included. Mr. Bentham, the very incarnation of his reason, has told him so.* And if he come to the pure reason of the Germans, or the discoveries which that contemplative nation say they have made in the highest regions of

* "Deontology," vol ii. p. 102.

the mind, of a reason *above* ordinary reason, reconciling the logic and consciousness of the latter with the former's instinctive and hitherto undeveloped affirmations, he is told that he may give evidence to faith after his own most approved fashion. For our parts, we confess that we are of a more child-like turn of contentment; and that, keeping our ordinary reason to what appears to us its fittest task,—namely, the guarding us against the admission of gratuitous pains,—we will suffer a loving faith to open to us whatever regions it pleases of possibilities honorable to God and man, cultivating them studiously, whether we thoroughly understand them or not. For who thoroughly understands any thing which he cultivates, even to the flowers at his feet? And, cultivating these, shall we refuse to cultivate also the stars, and aspirations and thoughts angelical, and hopes of rejoining friends and kindred, and all the flowers of heaven? No, assuredly,—not while we have a star to *see*, and a thought to reach it. Why should Heaven have given us those? Why not have put us into some blank region of space, with a wall of nothingness on all sides of us, and no power to have a thought beyond it? Because, some advocate of chance and blind action may say, it could not help it; because the nature of things could not help it; because things are as they are. Oh the assumptions of those who protest against assumption! of the faculty which exclusively calls itself reason, and would deprive us of some of our most reasonable faculties! Even upon the ground of these gentlemen's showing, faith itself cannot be helped; at least, not as long as things "are as they are;" and, in this respect, we are assuredly not for helping it. We are content to let it love and be happy.

With regard to the belief in spirits (which we take this opportunity of saying a few words upon, as it was in answer to our correspondent on this subject that we made use of the word we have explained), it has surely a right, even upon the severest grounds of reason, to rest upon the same privileges of possibility, and of a modest and wise ignorance to the contrary, as any other parts of a loving and even a knowing faith; for, the more we know of creation, the more we discover of the endless and thronging forms of it,—of the crowds in air, earth, and water: and are we, with our confessedly limited faculties, and our daily discoveries of things wonderful, to assume that there are no modes of being but such as are cognizable to our five senses? Had we possessed but two or three senses, we know very well that there are thousands of things round about us of which we could have formed no conception; and does not common modesty, as well as the possibilities of infinitude, demand of us that we should suppose there are senses besides our own, and that, with the help of but one more, we might become aware of phenomena at present unmanifested to human eyes? Locke has given celebrity to a story of a blind man, who, being asked what he thought of the color of red, said he conceived it must be like the sound of a trumpet. A counterpart to this story has been found (we know not with what truth) in that of a deaf man, who is said to have likened the sound of a trumpet to the color of red. Dr. Blacklock, who was blind from his infancy, and who wrote very good *heart* and *impart* verses, in which he talked of light and colors with all the confidence of a repetition-exercise, (a striking lesson to us verse-makers!) being requested one day to state what he really thought of something visible, — of the sun, for instance, — said, with modest hesitation, that he conceived it must resemble "*a pleasing friendship*"! We quote from memory; but this was his simile. We may thus judge what we miss by the small amount of our own complete senses. We may have been sometimes tempted to think, seeing what a beautiful world this is, and how little we make of it, that human beings are not the chief inhabitants of the planet, but that there are others, of a nobler sort, who see and enjoy all its loveliness, and who regard us with the same curiosity with which we look upon bees or beavers. But a consideration of the divine qualities of love and imagination and hope (as well as some other reflections, more serious) restores us to confidence in ourselves, and we resume our task of endeavoring to equalize enjoyment with the abundance afforded us. When we look upon the stars at night-time, shining and sparkling like so many happy eyes, conscious of their joy, we cannot help fancying that they are so many heavens, which have realized, or are in the progress of realizing, the perfections of which they are capable; and that our own planet (a star in the heavens to them) is one of the same golden brotherhood of hope and possibility, destined to be retained as a heaven, if its inhabitants answer to the incitements of the great Experimenter, or to be done away with for a new experiment if they fail. For endeavor and failure, in the particular, are manifestly a part of the universal system: and considering the large scale on which Providence acts, and the mixture of evil through which good advances, deluges are to be accounted for on principles of the most natural reason, moral as well as physical; and an awful belief thus becomes reconcilable to the commonest deductions of utility.

But "bad spirits" and spirits to be "afraid of"? We confess, that large and willing as our faith is in the utmost possibilities of life, and varieties of being, we see no reason of any sort to believe in those, at least not as made up of any thing like pure evil or malignity. It is possible that other beings, as well as men, may partake more or less of imperfection, and so be liable to mistake and brute impulses; but, as we need not be troubled with this side of spiritual possibility, why should we? For as to pure evil or malignity for its own sake, apart from some procurement or notion of good, nothing which we see in all nature induces us to suppose it possible. The veriest wretch that ever astonished the community did not perpetrate his crime out of sheer love of inflicting evil, but out of some false idea of good and pleasure, or of avoidance of evil; which idea might have been done away in him by a wiser and healthier training. And as to the belief in a great malignant principle, or Devil (though even he has his horrible story lightened by a mixture of mistake and suffering), the most devout Christians have long been giving it up, especially since they have observed that the places in which he is mentioned in Scripture are very rare, sometimes apocryphal, and at other times translatable into a very different sense from what was commonly received. In truth, the word "devil" has *not been translated at all;* it has simply been *repeated*, and thus given rise, in many instances, to a manifest and painful delusion; for *devil* (*diabolus*, Latin; *diavolo*, Italian) is merely the Greek word διαβολος (*diabolos*) repeated; and *diabolos* signified simply an accuser, — a calumniator: it was a Greek word for an evil speaker, a thrower of stones, and came from a verb signifying to *cast through* or *against*. The Latin word is used in the sense to this day, in the well-known appellation of the Attorney-General, which has caused so many jokes against that officer: for he who was known in France by the title of Public Accuser is designated in law Latin as the King's or Royal Accuser; that is to say, Devil, — "Diabolus Regis." The word is flat and plain enough, and very edifying. How simply is the frightful supernatural caution of the apostle thus converted into the most natural of all cautions! —

"Be sober, be vigilant" (says the *Greek*-English); "for your adversary the *Devil* walketh about, seeking whom he may devour."

But "Be sober, be vigilant" (says the proper *English*-English); "for your adversary the *Accuser* walketh about, seeking whom he may devour."

Here is a poor mistaken human being, instead of a prowling Satan; and what can be more natural, simple, or reconcilable with God's goodness and preeminence, and the working of an improvable weakness and blockish mystery, instead of a malignant might?

To show how accustomed we are to follow up the spiritual analogies suggested by all kinds of reasonable and loving faith, we will close this article with a copy of verses which we wrote last winter, after we had been thinking of some beloved friends who have disappeared from this present state of being: —

AN ANGEL IN THE HOUSE.

How sweet it were, if without feeble fright,
Or dying of the dreadful beauteous sight,
An angel came to us, and we could bear
To see him issue from the silent air
At evening in our room, and bend on ours
His divine eyes, and bring us from his bowers
News of dear friends, and children who have never
Been dead indeed! as we shall know for ever.
Alas! we think not what we daily see
About our hearths, — angels that *are* to be,
Or may be if they will, and we prepare
Their souls and ours to meet in happy air, —
A child, a friend, a wife whose soft heart sings
In unison with ours, breeding its future wings.

ON DEATH AND BURIAL.

THE cultivation of pleasant associations is, next to health, the great secret of enjoyment; and accordingly, as we lessen our cares and increase our pleasures, we may imagine ourselves affording a grateful spectacle to the Author of happiness. Error and misery, taken in their proportion, are the exceptions in his system. The world is most unquestionably happier, upon the whole, than otherwise; or light and air, and the face of Nature, would be different from what they are, and mankind no longer be buoyed up in perpetual hope and action. By cultivating agreeable thoughts, then, we tend, like bodies in philosophy, to the greater mass of sensations, rather than the less.

What we can enjoy, let us enjoy like creatures made for that very purpose: what we cannot, let us, in the same character, do our best to deprive of its bitterness. Nothing can be more idle than the voluntary gloom with which people think to please Heaven in certain matters, and which they confound with serious acknowledgment, or with what they call a due sense of its dispensations. It is nothing but the cultivation of the principle of fear, instead of confidence, with whatever name they may disguise it. It is carrying frightened faces to court, instead of glad and grateful ones;

and is above all measure ridiculous, because the real cause of it, and, by the way, of a thousand other feelings which religious courtiers mistake for religion, cannot be concealed from the Being it is intended to honor. There is a dignity certainly in suffering well, where we cannot choose but suffer; if we must take physic, let us do it like men: but what would be his dignity, who, when he had the choice in his power, should make the physic bitterer than it is, or even to refuse to render it more palatable, purely to look grave over it, and do honor to the physician?

The idea of our dissolution is one of those which we most abuse in this manner, principally, no doubt, because it is abhorrent from the strong principle of vitality implanted in us, and the habits that have grown up with it. But what then? So much the more should we divest it of all the unpleasant associations which it need not excite, and add to it all the pleasant ones which it will allow.

But what is the course we pursue? We remember having a strong impression, years ago, of the absurdity of our mode of treating a death-bed, and of the great desirableness of having it considered as nothing but a sick one, — one to be smoothed and comforted, even by cordial helps, if necessary. We remember also how some persons, who, nevertheless, did too much justice to the very freest of our speculations to consider them as profane, were startled by this opinion, till we found it expressed, in almost so many words, by no less an authority than Lord Bacon. We got at our notion through a very different process, no doubt, — he through the depth of his knowledge, and we from the very buoyancy of our youth; but we are not disposed to think it the less wise on that account. "The serious," of course, are bound to be shocked at so cheering a proposition; but of them we have already spoken. The great objection would be, that such a system would deprive the evil-disposed of one terror in prospect, and that this principle of determent is already found too feeble to afford any diminution. The fact is, the whole principle is worth little or nothing, unless the penalty to be inflicted is pretty certain, and appeals also to the less sentimental part of our nature. It is good habits, a well-educated conscience, a little early knowledge, the cultivation of generous motives, must supply people with preventives of bad conduct: their sense of things is too immediate and lively to attend, in the long-run, to any thing else. We will be bound to say, generally speaking, that the prospective terrors of a death-bed never influenced any others than nervous consciences, too weak, and inhabiting organizations too delicate, to afford to be very bad ones. But, in the mean time, they may be very alarming to such consciences in prospect, and very painful to the best and most temperate of mankind in actual sufferance; and why should this be, but, as we have said before, to keep bitter that which we could sweeten, and to persist in a mistaken want of relief, under a notion of its being a due sense of our condition? We know well enough what a due sense of our condition is in other cases of infirmity; and what is a death-bed but the very acme of infirmity, —the sickness, bodily and mental, that, of all others, has most need of relief?

If the death happens to be an easy one, the case is altered; and no doubt it is oftener so than people imagine: but how much pains are often taken to render it difficult! First, the chamber in which the dying person lies is made as gloomy as possible with curtains and vials and nurses and terrible whispers, and perhaps the continual application of handkerchiefs to weeping eyes; then, whether he wishes it or not, or is fit to receive it or not, he is to have the whole truth told him by some busy-body who never was so anxious, perhaps, in the cause of veracity before; and lastly come partings, and family assemblings, and confusion of the head with matters of faith, and trembling prayers, that tend to force upon dying weakness the very doubts they undertake to dissipate. Well may the soldier take advantage of such death-beds as these to boast of the end that awaits him in the field.

But, having lost our friend, we must still continue to add to our own misery at the circumstance. We must heap about the recollection of our loss all the most gloomy and distasteful circumstances we can contrive, and thus, perhaps, absolutely incline ourselves to think as little of him as possible. We wrap the body in ghastly habiliments; put it in as tasteless a piece of furniture as we can invent; dress ourselves in the gloomiest of colors; awake the barbarous monotony of the church-bell (to frighten every sick person in the neighborhood); call about us a set of officious mechanics of all sorts, who are counting their shillings, as it were, by the tears that we shed, and watching with jealousy every candle's end of their "perquisites;" and proceed to consign our friend or relation to the dust, under a ceremony that takes particular pains to impress that consummation on our minds. Lastly come tasteless tombstones and ridiculous epitaphs, with perhaps a skull and cross-bones at top; and the tombstones are crowded together, generally in the middle of towns, always near the places of worship, unless the church-yard is overstocked. Scarcely ever is there a tree on the spot: in some remote villages alone are the graves ever decorated with flowers.* All is stony, earthy, and dreary. It seems as if, after having rendered every thing before death as painful as possible, we endeavored to subside into a sullen indifference, which contradicted itself by its own efforts.

The Greeks managed these things better. It is curious that we, who boast so much of our knowledge of the immortality of the soul, and of the glad hopes of an after-life, should take such pains to make the image of death melancholy; while, on the other hand, Gentiles whom we treat with so much contempt for their ignorance on those heads should do the reverse, and associate it with emblems that ought to belong rather to us. But the truth is, that we know very little what we are talking about, when we speak, in the gross, of the ancients, and of their ideas of Deity and humanity. The very finest and most amiable part of our notions on those subjects comes originally from their philosophers: all the rest,— the gloom, the bad passions, the favoritism — are the work of other

* Matters have been improving since this article was written.

hands, who have borrowed the better materials as they proceeded, and then pretended an original right in them. Even the absurd parts of the Greek mythology are less painfully absurd than those of any other; because, generally speaking, they are on the cheerful side instead of the gloomy. We would rather have a Deity who fell in love with the beautiful creatures of his own making, than one who would consign nine hundred out of a thousand to destruction for not believing ill of him.

But not to digress from the main subject. The ancients did not render the idea of death so harshly distinct, as we do, from that of life. They did not extinguish all light and cheerfulness in their minds, and in things about them, as it were, on the instant; neither did they keep before one's eyes, with hypochondriacal pertinacity, the idea of death's-heads and skeletons, which, as representations of humanity, are something more absurd than the brick which the pedant carried about as the specimen of his house. They selected pleasant spots for sepulture, and outside the town; they adorned their graves with arches and pillars, — with myrtles, lilies, and roses; they kept up the social and useful idea of their great men by entombing them near the highway, so that every traveller paid his homage as he went; and, latterly, they reduced the dead body to ashes, — a clean and inoffensive substance — gathered it into a tasteful urn, and often accompanied it with other vessels of exquisite construction, on which were painted the most cheerful actions of the person departed, even to those of his every-day life, — the prize in the games, the toilet, the recollections of his marriages and friendships,—the figures of beautiful females,—every thing, in short, which seemed to keep up the idea of a vital principle, and to say, "The creature who so did, and so enjoyed itself, cannot be all gone." The image of the vital principle, and of an after-life, was, in fact, often and distinctly repeated on these vessels by a variety of emblems, animal and vegetable, particularly the image of Psyche, or the soul, by means of the butterfly,—an association which, in process of time, as other associations gathered about it, gave rise to the most exquisite allegory in the world,—the story of *Cupid* and *Psyche*.

Now, we do not mean to say that everybody who thinks as we do upon this subject should or can depart at once from existing customs, especially the chief ones. These things must either go out gradually, or by some convulsive movement in society, as others have gone; and mere eccentricity is no help to their departure. What we cannot undo, let us only do as decently as possible: but we might render the dying a great deal more comfortable by just daring a little to consider their comforts, and not our puerility; we might allow their rooms also to be more light and cheerful; we might take pains to bring pleasanter associations about them altogether; and, when they were gone, we might cultivate our own a little better; our tombstones might at least be in better taste; we might take more care of our graves; we might preserve our sick neighbors from the sound of the death-bell; a single piece of ribbon or crape would surely be enough to guard us against the unweeting inquiries of friends;

while, in the rest of our clothes, we might adopt, by means of a ring or a watch-ribbon, some cheerful instead of gloomy recollection of the person we had lost, — a favorite color, for instance, or device, — and thus contrive to balance a grief which we must feel, and which indeed, in its proper associations, it would not be desirable to avoid. Rousseau died gazing on the setting sun, and was buried under green trees. Petrarch, who seemed born to complete and render glorious the idea of an author from first to last, was found dead in his study, with his head placidly resting on a book. What is there in deaths like these to make us look back with anguish, or to plunge into all sorts of gloominess and bad taste?

We know not whether it has ever struck any of our readers, but we seem to consider the relics of ancient taste, which we possess, as things of mere ornament, and forget that their uses may be in some measure preserved, so as to complete the idea of their beauty, and give them, as it were, a soul again. We place their urns and vases, for instance, about our apartments, but never think of putting any thing in them; yet, when they are not absolutely too fragile, we might often do so, — fruit, flowers, toilet utensils, a hundred things, with a fine opportunity (to boot) of showing our taste in inscriptions. The Chinese, in the "Citizen of the World," when he was shown the two large vases from his own country, was naturally amused to hear that they only served to fill up the room, and held no supply of tea in them as they did at home. A lady, a friend of ours, who shows in her countenance her origin from a country of taste, and who acts up to the promise of her countenance, is the only person, but one, whom we ever knew to turn antique ornament to account in this respect. She buried a favorite bird in a vase on her mantel-piece; and there the little rogue lies, with more kind and tasteful associations about him than the greatest dust in Christendom. The other instance is that of two urns of marble, which have been turned as much as possible to the original purposes of such vessels by becoming the depository of locks of hair. A lock of hair is an actual relic of the dead; as much so, in its proportion, as ashes, and more lively and recalling than even those. It is the part of us that preserves vitality longest; it is a clean and elegant substance; and it is especially connected with ideas of tenderness, in the cheek or the eyes about which it may have strayed, and the handling we may have given it on the living head. The thoughts connected with such relics, time gradually releases from grief itself, and softens into tender enjoyment; and we know, that, in the instance alluded to, the possessor of those two little urns would no more consent to miss them from his study than he would any other cheerful association that he could procure. It is a consideration, which he would not forego for a great deal, that the venerable and lovely dust to which they belonged lies in a village church-yard, and has left the most unfading part of it enclosed in graceful vessels.

1814.

ON WASHER-WOMEN.

WRITERS, we think, might oftener indulge themselves in direct picture-making, that is to say, in detached sketches of men and things, which should be to *manners* what those of Theophrastus are to *character*.

Painters do not always think it necessary to paint epics, or to fill a room with a series of pictures on one subject. They deal sometimes in single figures and groups, and often exhibit a profounder feeling in these little concentrations of their art than in subjects of a more numerous description. Their *gusto*, perhaps, is less likely to be lost on that very account. They are no longer Sultans in a seraglio, but lovers with a favorite mistress, retired and absorbed. A Madonna of Correggio's, the Bath of Michael Angelo, the Standard of Leonardo da Vinci, Titian's Mistress, and other single subjects or groups of the great masters, are acknowledged to be among their greatest performances, some of them their greatest of all.

It is the same with music. Overtures, which are supposed to make allusion to the whole progress of the story they precede, are not always the best productions of the master; still less are choruses and quintets, and other pieces involving a multiplicity of actors. The overture to Mozart's *Magic Flute* (*Zauberflöte*) is worthy of the title of the piece; it is truly enchanting: but what are so intense, in their way, as the duet of the two lovers, *Ah, Perdona;* or the laughing trio in *Cosi Fan Tutte;* or that passionate serenade in Don Giovanni, *Deh vieni alla finestra*, which breathes the very soul of refined sensuality? The gallant is before you, with his mandolin and his cap and feather, taking place of the nightingale for that amorous hour; and you feel that the sounds must inevitably draw his mistress to the window. Their intenseness even renders them pathetic; and his heart seems in earnest, because his senses are.

We do not mean to say, that, in proportion as the work is large and the subject numerous, the merit may not be the greater if all is good. Raphael's Sacrament is a greater work than his Adam and Eve: but his Transfiguration would still have been the finest picture in the world, had the second group in the foreground been away; nay, the latter is supposed, and, we think, with justice, to injure its effect. We only say that there are times when the numerousness may scatter the individual gusto; that the greatest possible feeling may be proved without it; and, above all, returning to our more immediate subject, that writers, like painters, may sometimes have leisure for excellent detached pieces, when they want it for larger productions. Here, then, is an opportunity for them. Let them, in their intervals of history, or if they want time for it, give us portraits of humanity. People lament that Sappho did not wrote more; but, at any rate, her two odes are worth twenty epics like Tryphiodorus.

But, in portraits of this kind, writing will also have a great advantage, and may avoid what seems to be an inevitable stumbling-block in paintings of a similar description. Between the matter-of-fact works of the Dutch artists, and the subtle compositions of Hogarth, there seems to be a medium reserved only for the pen. The writer only can tell you all he means, — can let you into his whole mind and intention. The moral insinuations of the painter are, on the one hand, apt to be lost for want of distinctness; or tempted, on the other, by their visible nature, to put on too gross a shape. If he leaves his meanings to be imagined, he may unfortunately speak to unimaginative spectators, and generally does; if he wishes to explain himself so as not to be mistaken, he will paint a set of comments upon his own incidents and characters, rather than let them tell for themselves. Hogarth himself, for instance, who never does any thing without a sentiment or a moral, is too apt to perk them both in your face, and to be over-redundant in his combinations. His persons, in many instances, seem too much taken away from their proper indifference to effect, and to be made too much of conscious agents and joint contributors. He "o'er-informs his tenements." His very goods and chattels are didactic. He makes a capital remark of a cow's horn, and brings up a piece of cannon in aid of a satire on vanity.* It is the writer only, who, without hurting the most delicate propriety of the representation, can leave no doubt of all his

* See the cannon going off in the turbulent portrait of a general-officer, and the cow's head coming just over that of the citizen who is walking with his wife.

intentions; who can insinuate his object, in two or three words, to the dullest conception; and, in conversing with the most foreign minds, take away all the awkwardness of interpretation. What painting gains in universality to the eye, it loses by an infinite proportion in power of suggestion to the understanding.

There is something of the sort of sketches we are recommending in Sterne: but Sterne had a general connected object before him, of which the parts apparently detached were still connecting links; and while he also is apt to overdo his subject, like Hogarth, is infinitely less various and powerful. The greatest master of detached portrait is Steele; but his pictures, too, form a sort of link in a chain. Perhaps the completest specimen of what we mean in the English language is Shenstone's "School-mistress," by far his best production; and a most natural, quiet, and touching old dame. But what?—are we leaving out *Chaucer?* Alas! we thought to be doing something a little original, and find it all existing already, and in unrivalled perfection, in his portraits of the Canterbury Pilgrims. We can only dilate, and vary upon his principle.

But we are making a very important preface to what may turn out a very trifling subject; and must request the reader not to be startled at the homely specimen we are about to give him, after all this gravity of recommendation. Not that we would apologize for homeliness, as homeliness. The beauty of this unlimited power of suggestion in writing is, that you may take up the driest and most commonplace of all possible subjects, and strike a light out of it to warm your intellect and your heart by. The fastidious habits of polished life generally incline us to reject, as incapable of interesting us, whatever does not present itself in a graceful shape of its own and a ready-made suit of ornaments. But some of the plainest weeds become beautiful under the microsope. It is the benevolent provision of Nature, that, in proportion as you feel the necessity of extracting interest from common things, you are enabled to do so; and the very least that this familiarity with homeliness will do for us is to render our artificial delicacy less liable to annoyance, and to teach us how to grasp the nettles till they obey us.

The reader sees that we are Wordsworthians enough not to confine our tastes to the received elegances of society: and, in one respect, we go farther than Mr. Wordsworth; for, though as fond, perhaps, of the country as he, we can manage to please ourselves in the very thick of cities, and even find there as much reason to do justice to Providence as he does in the haunts of sportsmen and anglers and all-devouring insects.

To think, for instance, of that laborious and inelegant class of the community, — *washer-women;* and of all the hot, disagreeable, dabbing, smoking, splashing, kitcheny, cold-dining, anti-company-receiving associations to which they give rise. What can be more annoying to any tasteful lady or gentleman, at their first waking in the morning, than when that dreadful thump at the door comes, announcing the tub-tumbling viragoes, with their brawny arms and brawling voices? We must confess, for our own parts, that our taste, in the abstract, is not for washer-women: we prefer Dryads and Naiads, and the figures that resemble them,—

> "Fair forms, that glance amid the green of woods,
> Or from the waters give their sidelong shapes
> Half swelling."

Yet we have lain awake sometimes in a street in town, after this first confounded rap, and pleased ourselves with imagining how equally the pains and enjoyments of this world are dealt out, and what a pleasure there is in the mere contemplation of any set of one's fellow-creatures and their humors, when our knowledge has acquired humility enough to look at them steadily.

The reader knows the knock which we mean. It comes like a lump of lead, and instantly wakes the maid, whose business it is to get up, though she pretends not to hear it. Another knock is inevitable, and it comes, and then another; but still Betty does not stir, or stirs only to put herself in a still snugger posture, knowing very well that they must knock again. "Now, 'drat that Betty!" says one of the washer-women; "she hears as well as we do, but the deuse a bit will she move till we give her another:" and, at the word "another," down goes the knocker again. "It's very odd," says the master of the house, mumbling from under the bed-clothes, "that Betty does not get up to let the people in: I've heard that knocker three times."—"Oh!" returns the mistress, "she's as lazy as she's high,"—and off goes the chamber-bell: by which time, Molly, who begins to lose her sympathy with her fellow-servant in impatience of what is going on, gives her one or two conclusive digs in the side; when the other gets up, and rubbing her eyes, and mumbling, and hastening and shrugging herself down stairs, opens the door with, "Lard, Mrs. Watson, I hope you haven't been standing here long?"—"Standing here long, Mrs. Betty! Oh! don't tell me: people might stand starving their legs off, before you'd put a finger out of bed."—"Oh! don't say so, Mrs. Watson; I'm sure I always rises at the first knock: and there,—you'll find every thing comfortable below, with a nice hock of ham, which I made John leave for you." At this the washer-women leave their grumbling, and shuffle down stairs, hoping to see Mrs. Betty early at breakfast. Here, after warming themselves at the copper, taking a mutual pinch of snuff, and getting things ready for the wash, they take a snack at the promised hock; for people of this profession have always their appetite at hand, and every interval of labor is invariably cheered by the prospect of *having something* at the end of it. "Well," says Mrs. Watson, finishing the last cut, "some people thinks themselves mighty generous for leaving one what little they can't eat; but, howsomever, it's better than nothing." "Ah," says Mrs. Jones, who is a minor genius, "one must take what one can get now-a-days; but Squire Hervey's for my money."—"Squire Hervey!" rejoins Mrs. Watson: "what's that, the great what's-his-name as lives yonder?"—"Ay," returns Mrs. Jones; "him as has a niece and nevvy, as they say, eats him out of house and land." And here commences the history of all the last week of the whole neighborhood round, which continues amidst the dipping of splashing fists, the rumbling of suds, and the creaking of wringings-out, till an hour or two are elapsed; and then for another snack and a pinch of snuff, till the resumption of another hour's labor or so brings round the time for first breakfast. Then, having had nothing to signify since five, they sit down at half-past six in the wash-house to take their own meal before the servants meet at the general one. This is the chief moment of enjoyment. They have just labored enough to make the tea and bread and butter welcome; are at an interesting point of the conversation (for there they contrive to leave off on purpose); and so down they sit, fatigued and happy, with their red elbows and white corrugated fingers, to a tub turned upside down, and a dish of good Christian souchong, fit for a body to drink.

We could dwell a good deal upon this point of time, but shall only admonish the fastidious reader, who thinks he has all the taste and means of enjoyment to himself, how he looks with scorn upon two persons, who are perhaps at this moment the happiest couple of human beings in the street, — who have discharged their duty, have earned their enjoyment, and have health and spirits to relish it to the full. A washerwoman's cup of tea may vie with the first drawn cork at a bon-vivant's table, and the complacent opening of her snuff-box with that of the most triumphant politician over a scheme of partition. We say nothing of the continuation of their labors, of the scandal they resume, or the complaints they pour forth, when they first set off again in the indolence of a satisfied appetite, at the quantity of work which the mistress of the house, above all other mistresses, is sure to heap upon them. Scandal and complaint, in these instances, do not hurt the complacency of our reflections: they are in their proper sphere; and are nothing but a part, as it were, of the day's work, and are so much vent to the animal spirits. Even the unpleasant day which the work causes up stairs in some houses, the visitors which it excludes, and the leg of mutton which it hinders from roasting, are only so much enjoyment kept back and contrasted, in order to be made keener the rest of the week. Beauty itself is indebted to it, and draws from that steaming out-house and splashing tub the well-fitting robe that gives out its figure, and the snowy cap that contrasts its curls and its complexion. In short, whenever we hear a washerwoman at her foaming work, or see her plodding towards us with her jolly warm face, her mob cap, her black stockings, clattering pattens, and tub at arm's-length resting on her hip-joint, we look upon her as a living lesson to us to make the most both of time and comfort, and as a sort of allegorical compound of pain and pleasure, a little too much, perhaps, in the style of Rubens.

1814.

THE NIGHTMARE.

WE DO not hesitate to declare to the reader, even in this free-thinking age, that we are no small adept in the uses of the occult philosophy, as I shall thoroughly make manifest. Be it known, then, that we are sometimes favored with the visits of a nocturnal spirit, from whom we receive the most excellent lessons of wisdom. His appearance is not highly prepossessing; and the weight of his manner of teaching, joined to the season he chooses for that purpose, has in it something not a little tremendous: but the end of his instruction is the enjoyment of virtue; and, as he is conscious of the alarming nature of his aspect, he takes leave of the initiated the moment they reduce his lessons to practice. It is true, there are a number of foolish persons, who, instead of being grateful for his friendly offices, have affected to disdain them, in the hope of tiring him out, and thus getting rid of his disagreeable presence: but they could not have taken a worse method; for his benevolence is as unwearied as his lessons and appearances are formidable, and these unphilosophic scorners are only punished every night of their lives in consequence. If any curious person wishes to see him, the ceremony of summoning him to appear is very simple, though it varies according to the aspirant's immediate state of blood. With some, nothing more is required than the mastication of a few unripe plums, or a cucumber, just before midnight; others must take a certain portion of that part of a calf which is used for what are vulgarly called veal-cutlets; others, again, find the necessary charm in an omelet or an olio. For our part, we are so well acquainted with the different ceremonies, that, without any preparation, we have only to lie in a particular posture, and the spirit is sure to make its appearance. The figures under which it presents itself are various: but it generally takes its position upon the breast, in a shape altogether indescribable; and is accompanied with circumstances of alarm and obscurity, not a little resembling those which the philosophers underwent on their initiation into the Eleusinian and other mysteries. The first sensations you experience are those of a great oppression, and inability to move: these you endeavor to resist, but after an instant resign yourself to their control, or rather flatter yourself you will do so; for the sensation becomes so painful, that, in a moment, you struggle into another effort; and if in this effort you happen to move yourself, and cry out, the spirit is sure to be gone; for it detests a noise as heartily as a monk of La Trappe, a traveller in the Alps, or a thief. Could an intemperate person in this situation be but philosopher enough to give himself up to the spirit's influence for a few minutes, he would see his visitant to great advantage, and gather as much knowledge at once as would serve him instead of a thousand short visits, and make him a good liver for months to come.

It was by this method, some time ago, that we not only obtained a full view of the spirit, but, gradually gathering strength from sufferance, as those who are initiated into any great wisdom must, contrived to enter into conversation with it. The substance of our dialogue we hereby present to the reader; for it is a mistaken notion of the pretenders to the Cabala, that to reveal the secrets on these occasions is to do harm, and incur the displeasure of our spiritual acquaintances. All the harm is in not understanding the secrets properly, and explaining them for the benefit of mankind; and, on this head, we have an objection to make to that ancient and industrious order of illuminati, the Freemasons, who, though they hold, with our familiar, that eating suppers is one of the high roads to wisdom, differ with him in confining their knowledge to such persons as can purchase it.

We had returned at a late hour from the representation of a new comedy; and, after eating a sleepy and not very great supper, reclined ourself on the sofa in a half-sitting posture, and taken up a little "Horace" to see if we could keep our eyes open with a writer so full of contrast to what we had been hearing. We happened to pitch upon that ode, "At O Deorum quisquis," &c., describing an ancient witches' meeting; and fell into an obscure kind of revery upon the identity of popular superstitions in different ages and nations. The comic dramatist, however, had been too much for us; the weather, which had been warm, but was inclining to grow cloudy, conspired with our heaviness; and the only sounds to be heard were the ticking of a small clock in the room, and the fitful sighs of the wind as it rose without,—

"The moaning herald of a weeping sky."

By degrees our eyes closed, the hand with the book dropped one way, and the head dropped back the other upon a corner of the sofa.

When you are in a state the least adapted to bodily perception, it is well known that you are in the precise state for spiritual. We had not been settled, we suppose, for more than a quarter of an hour, when the lid of a veal-pie, which we had lately attacked, began swelling up and down with an extraordinary convulsion; and we plainly perceived a little figure rising from beneath it, which grew larger and larger as it ascended, and then advanced with great solemnity towards us over the dishes. This phenomenon, which we thought we had seen often before, but could not distinctly remember how or where, was about two feet high, six inches of which, at least, went to the composition of its head. Between its jaws and shoulders there was no separation whatever; so that its face, which was very broad and pale, came immediately on its bosom, where it quivered without ceasing in a very alarming manner, being, it seems, of a paralytic sensibility like blanc-mange. The fearfulness of this aspect was increased by two staring and intent eyes, a nose turned up, but large, and a pair of thick lips, turned despondingly down at the corners. Its hair, which stuck about its ears like the quills of a porcupine, was partly concealed by a bolster rolled into a turban, and decorated with duck's feathers. The body was dressed in a kind of armor, of a substance resembling what is called crackling; and girded with a belt curiously studded with Spanish olives, in the middle of which, instead of pistols, were stuck two small bottles containing a fiery liquor. On its shoulders were wings, shaped like a bat's, but much larger; its legs terminated in large feet of lead; and in its hands, which were of the same metal, and enormously disproportioned, it bore a Turkish bowstring.

At sight of this formidable apparition, we felt an indescribable and oppressive sensation, which by no means decreased as it came nearer and nearer, staring and shaking its face at us, and making as many ineffable grimaces as Munden in a farce. It was in vain, however, we attempted to move: we felt all the time like a leaden statue, or like Gulliver pinned to the ground by the Lilliputians; and was wondering how our sufferings would terminate, when the phantom, by a spring off the table, pitched himself with all his weight upon our breast, and, we thought, began fixing his terrible bowstring. At this, as we could make no opposition, we determined at least to cry out as lustily as possible; and were beginning to make the effort, when the spirit motioned us to be quiet, and, retreating a little from our throat, said, in a low, suffocating tone of voice, "Wilt thou never be philosopher enough to leave off sacrificing unto calf's flesh?"

"In the name of the Great Solomon's ring," we ejaculated, "what art thou?"

"My name," replied the being, a little angrily,

"which thou wast unwittingly going to call out, is Mnpvtglnau-auw-auww, and I am Prince of the Nightmares."

"Ah! my lord," returned we, "you will pardon our want of recollection; but we had never seen you in your full dress before, and your presence is not very composing to the spirits. Doubtless this is the habit in which you appeared with the other genii at the levee of the mighty Solomon."

"A fig for the mighty Solomon!" said the spirit good-humoredly: "this is the cant of the cabalists, who pretend to know so much about us. I assure you, Solomon trembled much more at me than I did at him. I found it necessary, notwithstanding all his wisdom, to be continually giving him advice; and many were the quarrels I had on his account with Peor, the Demon of Sensuality, and a female devil named Ashtoreth."

"The world, my prince," returned we, "do not give you credit for so much benevolence."

"No," quoth the vision: "the world are never just to their best advisers. My figure, it is true, is not the most prepossessing, and my manner of teaching is less so; but I am, nevertheless, a benevolent spirit, and would do good to the most ungrateful of your fellow-creatures. This very night, between the hours of ten and one, I have been giving lessons to no less than twelve priests and twenty-one citizens. The studious I attend somewhat later, and the people of fashion towards morning. But, as you seem inclined at last to make a proper use of my instructions, I will recount you some of my adventures, if you please, that you may relate them to your countrymen, and teach them to appreciate the trouble I have with them."

"You are really obliging," said we; "and we should be all attention, would you do us the favor to sit a little more lightly; for each of your fingers appears heavier than a porter's load; and, to say the truth, the very sight of that bowstring almost throttles us."

THE SUBJECT CONTINUED.

AT these words the spectre gave a smile, which we can compare to nothing but the effect of vinegar on a death's-head. However, he rose up, though very slowly; and we once more breathed with transport, like a person dropping into his chair after a long journey. He then seated himself with much dignity on the pillow, at the other end of the sofa, and thus resumed the discourse: "I have been among mankind ever since the existence of cooks and bad consciences; and my office is twofold,—to give advice to the well-disposed, and to inflict punishment on the ill. The spirits over which I preside are of that class called, by the ancients, Incubi: but it was falsely supposed that we were fond of your handsome girls, as the Rosicrucians maintain; for it is our business to suppress, not encourage, the passions, as you may guess by my appearance."

"Pardon us," interrupted we; "but the poets and painters represent your highness as riding about on horseback: some of them even make you the horse itself; and it is thus that we have been taught to account for the term nightmare."

Here the phantom gave another smile, which made us feel sympathetically about the mouth, as though one of our teeth was being drawn. "A pretty jest," said he: "as if a spiritual being had need of a horse to carry him! The general name of my species in this country is of Saxon origin. The Saxons, uniting as they did the two natures of Britons and Germans, ate and drank with a vengeance: of course they knew me very well; and, being continually visited by me in all my magnificence, called me, by way of eminence, the Night *Mara*, or Spirit of Night. As to the poets and painters, I do not know enough of them to be well acquainted with their misrepresentations of me; though all of those gentlemen who could afford it have been pretty intimate with me. The moralizing Epicurean, whom you have in your hand there, I knew very well. Very good things he wrote, to be sure, about temperance and lettuces; but he ate quite as good at Mecænas' table. You may see the delicate state of his faculties by the noise he makes about a little garlic. There was Congreve, too, who dined every day with a duchess, and had the gout: I visited him often enough, and once wreaked on him a pretty set of tortures under the figure of one Jeremy Collier. My Lord Rochester, who might have displayed so true a fancy of his own without my assistance, had scarcely a single idea with which I did not supply him for five years together; during which time, you know, he confessed himself to have been in a state of intoxication. But I am sorry to say that I have had no small trouble with some of your poetical moralists, as well as men of pleasure. Something, I confess, must be allowed to Pope, whose constitution disputed with him every hour's enjoyment; but an invalid so fond of good things might have spared the citizens and clergy a little. It must be owned, also, that the good temper he really possessed did much honor to his philosophy; but it would have been greater, could he have denied himself that silver saucepan. It seduced him into a hundred miseries. One night, in particular, I remember, after he had made a very sharp attack on Addison and a dish of lampreys, he was terribly used by my spirits, who appeared to him in the shapes of so many flying pamphlets: he awoke in great horror, crying out with a ghastly smile, like a man who pretends to go easily through a laborious wager, 'These things are my diversion.' As to your painters, I have known still less of them; though I am acquainted with one, now living, to whom I once sat at midnight for my portrait; and the likeness is allowed by all of us to be excellent."

"Well," interrupted we, "but it is not at all like you in your present aspect."

"No," replied the phantom: "it is my poetical look. I have all sorts of looks and shapes, — civic, political, and poetical. It is by particular favor that I appear to you as I really am; but, as you have not seen many of my shapes, I will, if you please, give you a sample of some of my best."

"Oh! by no means," said we, somewhat hastily: "we can imagine quite enough from your descriptions. The philosophers certainly ill used you when they represented you as a seducer."

"The false philosophers did," replied the spectre: "the real philosophers knew me better. It was at my instance that Pythagoras forbade the eating of beans.

Plato owed some of his schemes to my hints, though, I confess, not his best: and I also knew Socrates very well from my intimacy with Alcibiades; but the familiar that attended him was of a much higher order than myself, and rendered my services unnecessary. However, my veneration for that illustrious man was so great, that, on the night when he died, I revenged him finely on his two principal enemies. People talk of the flourishing state of vice, and the happiness which guilty people sometimes enjoy in contrast with the virtuous; but they know nothing of what they talk. You should have seen Alexander in bed after one of his triumphant feasts, or Domitian or Heliogabalus after a common supper, and you would have seen who was the true monarch, the master of millions, or the master of himself. The prince retired, perhaps amidst lights, garlands, and perfumes, with the pomp of music, and through a host of bowing heads. Every thing he saw and touched reminded him of empire. His bed was of the costliest furniture, and he reposed by the side of beauty. Reposed, did I say? As well might you stretch a man on a gilded rack, and fan him into forgetfulness. No sooner had he obtained a little slumber, but myself and other spirits revenged the crimes of the day: in a few minutes, the convulsive snatches of his hands and features announce the rising agitation; his face blackens and swells; his clinched hands grasp the drapery about him. He tries to turn, but cannot; for a hundred horrors, the least of which is of death, crowd on him, and wither his faculties; till at last, by an effort of despair, he wakes with a fearful outcry, and springs from the bed, pale, trembling, and aghast, afraid of the very assistance he would call, and terrified at the consciousness of himself. Such are the men before whom millions of you rational creatures consent to tremble."

"You talk like an orator," said we: "but surely every ambitious prince has not horrors like these; for every one is neither so luxurious as Alexander, nor so timid and profligate as a Domitian or Heliogabalus. Conquerors, one would think, are generally too full of business to have leisure for consciences and nightmares."

"Why, a great deal may be done," answered the spirit, "against horrors of any kind, by mere dint of industry. But too much business, especially of a nature that keeps passion on the stretch, will sometimes perform the office of indolence and luxury, and turn revengefully upon the mind. To this were owing, in great measure, the epilepsies of Cæsar and Mohammed. With the faces of most of the Roman emperors I am as familiar as an antiquary, particularly from Tiberius down to Caligula; and again from Constantine downwards. But, if I punished the degenerate Romans, I nevertheless punished their enemies too. They were not aware, when scourged by Attila, what nights their tormentor passed. Luckily for justice, he brought from Germany not only fire and sword, but a true German appetite. I know not a single conqueror of modern times who equalled him in horror of dreaming, unless it was a little, spare, aguey, peevish, supper-eating fellow, whom you call Frederick the Great. Those exquisite ragouts, the enjoyment of which added new relish to the sarcasms the latter dealt about him with a royalty so unanswerable, sufficiently revenged the sufferers for their submission. Nevertheless, he dealt by his dishes as some men do by their mistresses: he loved them the more they tormented him. Poor Trenck, with his bread and water in the dungeon of Magdeburg, enjoyed a repose fifty times more serene than the royal philosopher in his Palace of Sans Souci, or Without Care. Even on the approach of death, this great conqueror — this warrior full of courage and sage speculation — could not resist the customary pepper and sauce-piquante, though he knew he should inevitably see me at night, armed with all his sins, and turning his bed into a nest of monsters."

"Heaven be praised," cried we, "that he had a taste so retributive! The people under arbitrary governments must needs have a respect for the dishes at court. We now perceive, more than ever, the little insight we have into the uses of things. Formerly one might have imagined that eating and drinking had no use but the vulgar one of sustaining life; but it is manifest that they save the law a great deal of trouble, and the writers of cookery-books can be considered in no other light than as expounders of a criminal code. Really, we shall hereafter approach a dish of turtle with becoming awe, and already begin to look upon a ragout as something very equitable and inflexible."

"You do justice," observed the spirit, "to those eminent dishes, and in the only proper way. People who sit down to a feast with their joyous darting of eyes, and rubbing of hands, would have very different sensations did they know what they were about to attack. You must know that the souls of tormented animals survive after death, and become instruments of punishment for mankind. Most of these are under my jurisdiction, and form great part of the monstrous shapes that haunt the slumbers of the intemperate. Fish crimped alive, lobsters boiled alive, and pigs whipped to death, become the most active and formidable spirits; and, if the object of their vengeance take too many precautions to drown his senses when asleep, there is the subtle and fell gout waiting to torment his advanced years, — a spirit partaking of the double nature of the nightmare and salamander; and more terrible than any one of us, inasmuch as he makes his attacks by day as well as by night."

"We shudder to think," interrupted we, "even of the monstrous combinations which have disturbed our own rest, and formed so horrible a contrast to the gayety of a social supper."

"Oh! as for that matter," said the phantom, in a careless tone, "you know nothing of the horrors of a glutton or a nefarious debauchee. Suffocation with bolsters, heaping of rocks upon the chest, buryings alive, and strugglings to breathe without a mouth, are among their commonplace sufferings. The dying glutton, in La Fontaine, never was so reasonable as when he desired to have the remainder of his fish. He was afraid, that, if he did not immediately go off, he might have a nap before he died, which would have been a thousand times worse than death. Had Apicius, Ciacco the Florentine, Dartineuf, or Vitellius, been able and inclined to paint what they had seen, Callot would have been a mere Cipriani to them. I could produce you a jolly fellow, a corpulent nobleman, from the next hotel, the very counterpart of the glutton in Rubens's *Fall of the Damned*, who could bring together a more hideous combination of fancies than are to be found in Milton's hell. He is not without information, and a disposition naturally good: but a long series of bad habits have made him what they call a man of pleasure; that is to say, he takes all sorts of pains to get a little enjoyment which shall produce him a world of misery. One of his passions, which he *will* not resist, is for a particular dish, pungent, savory, and multifarious, which sends him almost every night into Tartarus. At this minute, the spectres of the supper-table are busy with him; and Dante himself could not have worked up a greater horror for the punishment of vice than the one he is undergoing. He fancies, that, though he is *himself*, he is nevertheless four different beings at once, of the most odious and contradictory natures; that his own indescribable feelings are fighting bodily and maliciously with each other; and that there is no chance left him, either for escape, forgetfulness, or cessation."

"Gracious powers!" cried we: "what, all this punishment for a dish?"

"You do not recollect," answered the spirit, "what an abuse such excesses are of the divine gift of reason, and how they distort the best tendencies of human nature. The whole end of existence is perverted by not taking proper care of the body. This man will rise to-morrow morning, pallid, nervous, and sullen: his feelings must be re-enforced with a dram to bear the ensuing afternoon; and I foresee that the ill-temper arising from his debauch will lead him into a very serious piece of injustice against his neighbor. To the same cause may be traced fifty of the common disquietudes of life, its caprices and irritabilities. To-night a poor fellow is fretful because his supper was not rich enough; but to-morrow night he will be in torture because it was too rich. An hysterical lady shall flatter herself she is sentimentally miserable, when most likely her fine feelings are to be deduced, not from sentiment, but a surfeit. Your Edinburgh wits thought they had laid down a very droll impossibility, when they talked of cutting a man's throat with a pound of pickled salmon; whereas much less dishes have performed as wonderful exploits. I have known a hard egg to fill a household with dismay for days together; a cucumber has disinherited an only son; and a whole province has incurred the royal anger of its master at the instigation of a set of woodcocks."

"It is a thousand pities," said we, "that history, instead of habituating us to love 'the pomp and circumstance' of bad passions, cannot trace the actions of men to their real sources."

"Well, well," said the spirit, "now that you are getting grave on the subject, I think I may bid you adieu. Your nation has produced excellent philosophers, who were not the less wise for knowing little of me. Pray, tell your countrymen that they are neither philosophic nor politic in feasting as they do on all occasions, joyful, sorrowful, or indifferent; that good sense, good temper, and the good of their country, are distinct things from indigestion; and that, when they think to show their patriotic devotion by carving and gormandizing, they are no wiser than the bacchanals of old, who took serpents between their teeth, and tortured themselves with knives."

So saying, the spectre rose, and stretching out his right hand, with a look which we believe he intended to be friendly, advanced towards us: he then took our hand in his own, and, perceiving signs of alarm in our countenance, burst into a fit of laughter, which was the very quintessence of discord, and baffles all description; being a compound of the gabblings of geese, grunting of hogs, quacking of ducks, squabbling of turkeys, and winding-up of smoke-jacks. When the fit was pretty well over, he gave us a squeeze of the hand, which made us jump up with a spring of the knees; and, gradually enveloping himself in a kind of steam, vanished with a noise like the crash of crockery-ware. We looked about us: we found that our right hand, which held the "Horace," had got bent under us, and gone to sleep; and that, in our sudden start, we had kicked half the dishes from the supper-table.

1811.

THE FLORENTINE LOVERS.*

AT the time when Florence was divided into the two fierce parties of Guelphs and Ghibellines, there was great hostility between two families of the name of Bardi and Buondelmonti. It was seldom that love took place between individuals of houses so divided; but, when it did, it was proportionately vehement, either because the individuals themselves were vehement in all their passions, or because love, falling upon two gentle hearts, made them the more pity and love one another to find themselves in so unnatural a situation.

Of this latter kind was an affection that took place between a young lady of the family of the Bardi, called Dianora d'Amerigo, and a youth of the other family, whose name was Ippolito. The girl was about fifteen, and in the full flower of her beauty and sweetness. Ippolito was about three years older, and looked two or three more, on account of a certain gravity and deep regard in the upper part of his face. You might know by his lips that he could love well, and by his eyes that he could keep the secret. There

* The groundwork of this story is in a late Italian publication, called the "Florentine Observer," descriptive of the old buildings, and other circumstances of local interest, in the capital of Tuscany.

was a likeness, as sometimes happens, between the two lovers; and perhaps this was no mean help to their passion: for as we find painters often giving their own faces to their heroes, so the more excusable vanity of lovers delights to find that resemblance in one another which Plato said was only the divorced half of the original human being rushing into communion with the other.

Be this as it may (and lovers in those times were not ignorant of such speculations), it needed but one sight of Dianora d'Amerigo to make Ippolito fall violently in love with her. It was in church on a great holiday. In the South, the church has ever been the place where people fall in love. It is there that the young of both sexes oftenest find themselves in each other's company. There the voluptuous, that cannot fix their thoughts upon heaven, find congenial objects, more earthly, to win their attention; and there the most innocent and devotional spirits, voluptuous also without being aware of it, and not knowing how to vent the grateful pleasure of their hearts, discover their tendency to repose on beings that can show themselves visibly sensible to their joy. The paintings, the perfumes, the music, the kind crucifix, the mixture of aspiration and earthly ceremony, the draperies, the white vestments of young and old, the boys' voices, the giant candles, typical of the seraphic ministrants about God's altar, the meeting of all ages and classes, the echoings of the aisles, the lights and shades of the pillars and vaulted roofs, the very struggle of daylight at the lofty windows, as if earth were at once present and not present, — all have a tendency to confuse the boundaries of this world and the next, and to set the heart floating in that delicious mixture of elevation and humility, which is ready to sympathize with whatever can preserve to it something like its sensations, and save it from the hardness and definite folly of ordinary life. It was in a church that Boccaccio — not merely the voluptuous Boccaccio, who is but half known by the half-witted, but Boccaccio the future painter of the Falcon and the Pot of Basil — first saw the beautiful face of his Fiammetta. In a church, Petrarch felt the sweet shadow fall on him that darkened his life for twenty years after. And the fond gratitude of the local historian for a tale of true love has left it on record, that it was in the Church of St. Giovanni at Florence, and on the great day of Pardon, which falls on the 13th of January, that Ippolito de' Buondelmonte became enamoured of Dianora d'Amerigo. [How delicious it is to repeat these beautiful Italian names, when they are not merely names! We find ourselves almost unconsciously writing them in a better hand than the rest; not merely for the sake of the printer, but for the pleasure of lingering upon the sound.]

When the people were about to leave church, Ippolito, in turning to speak to an acquaintance, lost sight of his unknown beauty. He made haste to plant himself at the door, telling his companion that he should like to see the ladies come out; for he had not the courage to say which lady. When he saw Dianora appear, he changed color, and saw nothing else. Yet though he beheld, and beheld her distinctly, so as to carry away every feature in his heart, it seemed to him afterwards that he had seen her only as in a dream. She glided by him like a thing of heaven, drawing her veil over her head. As he had not the courage to speak of her, he had still less the courage to ask her name; but he was saved the trouble. "God and St. John bless her beautiful face!" cried a beggar at the door: "she always gives double of any one else." — "Curse her!" muttered Ippolito's acquaintance: "she is one of the Bardi." The ear of the lover heard both these exclamations, and they made an indelible impression. Being a lover of books and poetry, and intimate with the most liberal of the two parties, such as Dante Alighieri (afterwards so famous) and Guido Cavalcanti, Ippolito, though a warm partisan himself, and implicated in a fierce encounter that had lately taken place between some persons on horseback, had been saved from the worst feelings attendant on political hostility; and they now appeared to him odious. He had no thought, it is true, of forgiving one of the old Bardi, who had cut his father down from his horse; but he would now have sentenced the whole party to a milder banishment than before; and to curse a female belonging to it, and that female Dianora! — he differed with the stupid fellow that had done it, whenever they met afterwards.

It was a heavy reflection to Ippolito to think that he could not see his mistress in her own house. She had a father and mother living as well as himself, and was surrounded with relations. It was a heavier still that he knew not how to make her sensible of his passion; and the heaviest of all, that, being so lovely, she would certainly be carried off by another husband. What was he to do? He had no excuse for writing to her; and as to serenading her under her window, unless he meant to call all the neighbors to witness his temerity, and lose his life at once in that brawling age, it was not to be thought of. He was obliged to content himself with watching, as well as he could, the windows of her abode; following her about whenever he saw her leave it, and with pardonable vanity trying to catch her attention by some little action that should give her a good thought of the stranger, — such as anticipating her in giving alms to a beggar. We must even record, that, on one occasion, he contrived to stumble against a dog, and tread on his toes, in order that he might ostentatiously help the poor beast out of the way. But his day of delight was church-day. Not a fast, not a feast, did he miss; not a Sunday, nor a saint's-day. "The devotion of that young gentleman," said an old widow-lady, her aunt, who was in the habit of accompanying Dianora, "is indeed edifying; and yet he is a mighty pretty youth, and might waste his time in sins and vanities with the gayest of them." And the old widow-lady sighed, doubtless out of a tender pity for the gay. Her recommendation of Ippolito to her niece's notice would have been little applauded by her family; but, to say the truth, she was not responsible. His manœuvres and constant presence had already gained Dianora's attention; and, with all the unaffected instinct of an Italian, she was not long in suspecting who it was that attracted his devotions, and in wishing very heartily that they might continue. She longed to learn who he was, but felt the same want of courage as he himself had experienced. "Did you observe," said the aunt, one day after leaving church, "how the poor boy blushed because he did but catch my eye? Truly, such modesty is very rare."—"Dear aunt," replied Dianora with a mixture of real and affected archness, of pleasure and of gratitude, "I thought you never wished me to notice the faces of young men."—"Not of young men, niece," returned the aunt gravely; "not of persons of twenty-eight or thirty, or so; nor indeed of youths in general, however young: but then this youth is very different; and the most innocent of us may look, once in a way or so, at so very modest and respectful a young gentleman. I say, respectful; because, when I gave him a slight courtesy of acknowledgment or so for making way for me in the aisle, he bowed to me with so solemn and thankful an air, as if the favor had come from me; which was extremely polite: and if he is very handsome, poor boy! how can he help that? Saints have been handsome in their days, ay, and young, or their pictures are not at all like, which is impossible; and I am sure St. Dominic himself, in the wax-work, God forgive me! hardly looks sweeter and humbler at the Madonna and Child than he did at me and you as we went by."—"Dear aunt," rejoined Dianora, "I did not mean to reproach you, I'm sure: but, sweet aunt! we do not know him, you know; and you know"— "Know!" cried the old lady: "I'm sure I know him as well as if he were my own aunt's son; which might not be impossible, though she is a little younger than myself; and, if he were my own, I should not be ashamed." — "And who, then," inquired Dianora, scarcely articulating her words, — "who, then, is he?"—"Who?" said the aunt: "why, the most edifying young gentleman in all Florence, that's who he is; and it does not signify what he is else, manifestly being a gentleman as he is, and one of the noblest, I warrant; and I wish you may have no worse husband, child, when you come to marry; though there is time enough to think of that. Young ladies, now-a-days, are always for knowing who everybody is, who he is, and what he is, and whether he is this person or that person, and is of the Grand Prior's side, or the Archbishop's side, and what not; and all this before they will allow him to be even handsome; which, I am sure, was not so in my youngest days. It is all right and proper, if matrimony is concerned, or they are in danger of marrying below their condition, or a profane person, or one that's hideous, or a heretic; but to admire an evident young saint, and one that never misses church, Sunday or saint's-day, or any day for aught that I see, is a thing, that, if any thing, shows we may hope for the company of young saints hereafter; and, if so very edifying a young gentleman is also respectful to the ladies, was not the blessed St. Francis himself of his opinion in that matter? And did not the seraphical St. Teresa admire him the more for it? And does not St. Paul, in his very epistles, send his best respects to the ladies Tryphœna and Tryphosa? And was there ever woman in the New Testament (with reverence be it spoken, if we may say women of such blessed females), —was there ever woman, I say, in the New

Testament, not even excepting Madonna Magdalen, who had been possessed with seven devils (which is not so many by half as some ladies I could mention), nor Madonna, the other poor lady, whom the unforgiving hypocrites wanted to stone" (and here the good old lady wept, out of a mixture of devotion and gratitude), — "was there one of all these women, or any other, whom our blessed Lord himself" (and here the tears came into the gentle eyes of Dianora) "did not treat with all that sweetness and kindness and tenderness and brotherly love, which, like all his other actions, and as the seraphical Father Antonio said the other day in the pulpit, proved him to be not only from heaven, but the truest of all nobles on earth, and a natural gentleman born?"

We know not how many more reasons the good old lady would have given, why all the feelings of poor Dianora's heart, not excepting her very religion, which was truly one of them, should induce her to encourage her affection for Ippolito. By the end of this sentence they had arrived at their home, and the poor youth returned to his. We say "poor" of both the lovers; for, by this time, they had both become sufficiently enamoured to render their cheeks the paler for discovering their respective families, which Dianora had now done as well as Ippolito.

A circumstance on the Sunday following had nearly discovered them, not only to one another, but to all the world. Dianora had latterly never dared to steal a look at Ippolito, for fear of seeing his eyes upon her; and Ippolito, who was less certain of her regard for him than herself, imagined that he had somehow offended her. A few Sundays before, she had sent him home bounding for joy. There had been two places empty where he was kneeling,—one near him, and the other a little farther off. The aunt and the niece, who came in after him, and found themselves at the spot where he was, were perplexed which of the two places to choose; when it seemed to Ippolito, that, by a little movement of her arm, Dianora decided for the one nearest him. He had also another delight. The old lady, in the course of the service, turned to her niece, and asked her why she did not sing as usual. Dianora bowed her head; and, in a minute or two afterwards, Ippolito heard the sweetest voice in the world, low indeed, almost to a whisper, but audible to him. He thought it trembled; and he trembled also. It seemed to thrill within his spirit in the same manner that the organ thrills through the body. No such symptom of preference occurred afterwards. The ladies did not come so near him, whatever pains he took to occupy so much room before they came in, and then make room when they appeared. However, he was self-satisfied as well as ingenious enough in his reasonings on the subject not to lay much stress upon this behavior, till it lasted week after week, and till he never again found Dianora looking even towards the quarter in which he sat: for it is our duty to confess, that if the lovers were two of the devoutest of the congregation, which is certain, they were apt also, at intervals, to be the least attentive; and, furthermore, that they would each pretend to look towards places at a little distance from the desired object, in order that they might take in, with the sidelong power of the eye, the presence and look of one another. But, for some time, Dianora had ceased even to do this; and though Ippolito gazed on her the more steadfastly, and saw that she was paler than before, he began to persuade himself that it was not on his account. At length, a sort of desperation urged him to get nearer to her, if she would not condescend to come near himself; and on the Sunday in question, scarcely knowing what he did, or how he saw, felt, or breathed, he knelt right down beside her. There was a pillar next him, which luckily kept him somewhat in the shade; and, for a moment, he leaned his forehead against the cold marble, which revived him. Dianora did not know he was by her. She did not sing; nor did the aunt ask her. She kept one unaltered posture, looking upon her mass-book; and he thought she did this on purpose. Ippolito, who had become weak with his late struggles of mind, felt almost suffocated with his sensations. He was kneeling side by side with her: her idea, her presence, her very drapery, which was all that he dared to feel himself in contact with, the consciousness of kneeling with her in the presence of Him whom tender hearts implore for pity on their infirmities, all rendered him intensely sensible of his situation. By a strong effort, he endeavored to turn his self-pity into a feeling entirely religious; but, when he put his hands together, he felt the tears ready to gush away so irrepressibly, that he did not dare it. At last, the aunt, who had in fact looked about for him, recognized him with some surprise, and more pleasure. She had begun to suspect his secret; and though she knew who he was, and that the two families were at variance, yet a great deal of good nature, a sympathy with pleasures of which no woman had tasted more, and some considerable disputes she had lately with another old lady, her kinswoman, on the subject of politics, determined her upon at least giving the two lovers that sort of encouragement which arises not so much from any decided object we have in view, as from a certain vague sense of benevolence, mixed with a lurking wish to have our own way. Accordingly, the well-meaning old widow-lady, without much consideration, and loud enough for Ippolito to hear, whispered her niece to let the gentleman next her read in her book, as he seemed to have forgotten to bring his own. Dianora, without lifting her eyes, and never suspecting who it was, moved her book sideways, with a courteous inclination of the head, for the gentleman to take it. He did so. He held it with her. He could not hinder his hand from shaking; but Dianora's reflections were so occupied upon one whom she little thought so near her, that she did not perceive it. At length, the book tottered so in his hand, that she could not but notice it. She turned to see if the gentleman was ill, and instantly looked back again. She felt that she herself was too weak to look at him; and whispering to her aunt, "I am very unwell," the ladies rose, and made their way out of the church. As soon as she felt the fresh air, she fainted, and was carried home; and it happened at the same moment, that Ippolito, unable to keep his feelings to himself, leaned upon the marble pillar at which he was kneeling, and groaned aloud. He fancied she had left him in disdain. Luckily for him, a circumstance of this kind was not unknown in a place where penitents would sometimes be overpowered by a sense of their crimes; and, though Ippolito was recognized by some, they concluded he had not been the innocent person they supposed. They made up their minds in future that his retired and bookish habits, and his late evident suffering, were alike the result of some dark offence; and, among these persons, the acquaintance who had cursed Dianora when he first beheld her was glad to be one; for without knowing his passion for her, much less her return of it, which was more than the poor youth knew himself, he envied him for his accomplishments and popularity.

Ippolito dragged himself home, and after endeavoring to move about for a day or two, and to get as far as Dianora's abode, — an attempt he gave up, for fear of being unable to come away again, — was fairly obliged to take to his bed. What a mixture of delight with sorrow would he have felt, had he known that his mistress was almost in as bad a state! The poor aunt, who soon discovered her niece's secret, now found herself in a dreadful dilemma; and the worst of it was, that being on the female side of the love, and told by Dianora that it would be the death of her if she disclosed it to "*him*," or anybody connected with him, or, indeed, anybody at all, she did not know what steps to take. However, as she believed that at least death might possibly ensue if the dear young people were not assured of each other's love, and certainly did not believe in any such mortality as her niece spoke of, she was about to make her first election out of two or three measures which she was resolved upon taking, when, luckily for the salvation of Dianora's feelings, she was surprised by a visit from the person whom of all persons in the world she wished to see, — Ippolito's mother.

The two ladies soon came to a mutual understanding, and separated with comfort for their respective patients. We need not wait to describe how a mother came to the knowledge of her son's wishes; nor will it be necessary to relate how delighted the two lovers were to hear of one another, and to be assured of each other's love. But Ippolito's illness now put on a new aspect; for the certainty of his being welcome to Dianora, and the easiness with which he saw his mother give way to his inclinations, made him impatient for an interview. Dianora was afraid of encountering him as usual in public; and he never ceased urging his mother till she consented to advise with Dianora's aunt upon what was to be done. Indeed, with the usual weakness of those who take any steps, however likely to produce future trouble, rather than continue a present uneasiness, she herself thought it high time to do something for the poor boy; for the house began to remark on his strange conduct. All his actions were either too quick or too slow. At one time he would start up to perform the most trivial office of politeness, as if he were going to stop a conflagration; at another, the whole world might move before him without his noticing. He would now leap on his horse, as if the enemy were at the city-gates; and next day, when going to mount it, stop on a sudden, with the reins in his hands, and fall a-musing.

"What is the matter with the boy?" said his father, who was impatient at seeing him so little his own master: "has he stolen a box of jewels?" for somebody had spread a report that he gambled, and it was observed that he never had any money in his pocket. The truth is, he gave it all away to the objects of Dianora's bounty, particularly to the man who blessed her at the church-door. One day, his father, who loved a bitter joke, made a young lady, who sat next him at dinner, lay her hand before him, instead of the plate; and, upon being asked why he did not eat, he was very near taking a piece of it for a mouthful. "Oh, the gallant youth!" cried the father; and Ippolito blushed up to the eyes, which was taken as a proof that the irony was well founded. But Ippolito thought of Dianora's hand, how it held the book with him when he knelt by her side; and, after a little pause, he turned, and took up that of the young lady, and begged her pardon with the best grace in the world. "He has the air of a prince," thought his father, "if he would but behave himself like other young men." The young lady thought he had the air of a lover; and, as soon as the meal was over, his mother put on her veil, and went to seek a distant relation called Gossip Veronica.

Gossip Veronica was in a singular position with regard to the two families of Bardi and Buondelmonti. She happened to be related at nearly equal distances to them both; and she hardly knew whether to be prouder of the double relationship, or more annoyed with the evil countenances they showed her, if she did not pay great attention to one of them, and no attention to the other. The pride remained uppermost, as it is apt to do; and she hazarded all consequences for the pleasure of inviting, now some of the young Bardi, and now some of the young Buondelmonti; hinting to them, when they went away, that it would be as well for them not to say that they had heard any thing of the other family's visiting her. The young people were not sorry to keep the matter as secret as possible, because their visits to Gossip Veronica were always restrained for a long time, if any thing of the sort transpired; and thus a spirit of concealment and intrigue was sown in their young minds, which might have turned out worse for Ippolito and Dianora, if their hearts had not been so good.

But here was a situation for Gossip Veronica! Dianora's aunt had been with her some days, hinting that something extraordinary, but as she hoped not unpleasant, would be proposed to the good Gossip, which for her part had her grave sanction; and now came the very mother of the young Buondelmonte to explain to her what this intimation was, and to give her an opportunity of having one of each family in her house at the same time! There was a great falling-off in the beatitude, when she understood that Ippolito's presence was to be kept a secret from all her visitors that day, except Dianora; but she was reconciled on receiving an intimation, that, in future, the two ladies would have no objection to her inviting whom she pleased to her house, and upon receiving a jewel from each of them as a pledge of their esteem. As to keeping the main secret, it was necessary for all parties.

Gossip Veronica, for a person in her rank of life, was rich, and had a pleasant villa at Monticelli, about half a mile from the city. Thither, on a holiday in September, which was kept with great hilarity by the peasants, came Dianora d'Amerigo de' Bardi, attended by her aunt Madonna Lucrezia, to see, as her mother observed, that no "improper persons" were there; and thither, before daylight, let in by Gossip Veronica herself, at the hazard of her reputation and of the furious jealousy of a young vine-dresser in the neighborhood, who loved her good things better than any thing in the world, except her waiting-maid, came the young Ippolito Buondelmonte de' Buondelmonti, looking, as she said, like the morning-star.

The morning-star hugged, and was hugged with great good-will by the kind Gossip, and then twinkled with impatience from a corner of her chamber-window till he saw Dianora. How his heart beat when he beheld her coming up through the avenue! Veronica met her near the garden-gate, and pointed towards the window as they walked along. Ippolito fancied she spoke of him, but did not know what to think of it; for Dianora did not change countenance, nor do any thing but smile good-naturedly on her companion, and ask her apparently some common question. The truth was, she had no suspicion he was there; though the Gossip, with much smirking and mystery, said she had a little present there for her, and such as her lady-mother approved. Dianora, whom, with all imaginable respect for her, the Gossip had hitherto treated, from long habit, like a child, thought it was some trifle or other, and forgot it next moment. Every step which Ippolito heard on the stair-case he fancied was hers, till it passed the door; and never did morning appear to him at once so delicious and so tiresome. To be in the same house with her, what joy! But to be in the same house with her, and not to be able to tell her his love directly, and ask her for hers, and fold her into his very soul, what impatience and misery! Two or three times, there was a knock of some one to be let in; but it was only the Gossip, come to inform him that he must be patient, and that she did not know when Madonna Lucrezia would please to bring Dianora, but most likely after dinner, when the visitors retired to sleep a little. Of all impertinent things, dinner appeared to him the most tiresome and unfit. He wondered how any thinking beings, who might take a cake or a cup of wine by the way, and then proceed to love one another, could sit round a great wooden table, patiently eating of this and that nicety; and, above all, how they could sit still afterwards for a moment, and not do any thing else in preference, — stand on their heads, or toss the dishes out of window. Then the festival! God only knew how happy the peasantry might choose to be, and how long they might detain Dianora with their compliments, dances, and songs. Doubtless there must be many lovers among them; and how they could bear to go jigging about in this gregarious manner, when they must all wish to be walking two by two in the green lanes, was to him inexplicable. However, Ippolito was very sincere in his gratitude to Gossip Veronica, and even did his best to behave handsomely to her cake and wine; and, after dinner, his virtue was rewarded.

It is unnecessary to tell the reader that he must not judge of other times and countries by his own. The real fault of those times, as of most others, lay, not in people's loves, but their hostilities; and, if both were managed in a way somewhat different from our own, perhaps neither the loves were less innocent, nor the hostilities more ridiculous. After dinner, when the other visitors had separated here and there to sleep, Dianora, accompanied by her aunt and Veronica, found herself, to her great astonishment, in the same room with Ippolito; and in a few minutes after their introduction to each other, and after one had looked this way, and the other that, and one taken up a book and laid it down again, and both looked out of the window, and each blushed, and either turned pale, and the gentleman adjusted his collar, and the lady her sleeve, and the elder ladies had whispered one another in a corner, Dianora, less to her astonishment than before, was left in the room with him alone. She made a movement as if to follow them; but Ippolito said something she knew not what, and she remained. She went to the window, looking very serious and pale, and not daring to glance towards him. He intended instantly to go to her, and wondered what had become of his fierce impatience; but the very delay had now something delicious in it. Oh the happiness of those moments! oh the sweet morning-time of those feelings! the doubt which is not doubt, and the hope which is but the coming of certainty! Oh, recollections enough to fill faded eyes with tears of renovation, and to make us forget we are no longer young, the next young and innocent beauty we behold! Why do not such hours make us as immortal as they are divine? Why are we not carried away, literally, into some place where they can last for ever; leaving those who miss us to say, "They were capable of loving, and they are gone to heaven"?

Reader. But, sir, in taking these heavenly flights of yours, you have left your two lovers.

Author. Surely, madam, I need not inform you that lovers are fond of being left, — at least to themselves.

Reader. But, sir, they are Italians; and I do not think Italian lovers were of this bashful description. I imagined, that, the moment your two Florentines beheld one another, they would spring into each other's arms, sending up cries of joy, and — and —

Author. Tumbling over the two old women by the way. It is a very pretty imagination, madam: but Italians partake of all the feelings common to human nature; and modesty is really not confined to the English, even though they are always saying it is.

Reader. But I was not speaking of modesty, sir: I was only alluding to a sort of — what shall I say? — a kind of irrepressible energy, that which in the Italian character is called violence.

Author. I meant nothing personal, madam, believe me, in using the word "modesty." You are too charitable, and have too great a regard for my lovers. I was not speaking myself of modesty in any particular sense, but of modesty in general; and all nations, not excepting our beloved and somewhat dictatorial countrymen, have their modesties and immodesties too, from which perhaps their example might instruct one another. With regard to the violence you speak of, and which is energy sometimes, and the weakest of weaknesses at others, according to the character which exhibits it, and the occasion that calls it forth, the Italians, who live in an ardent climate, have undoubtedly shown more of it than most people; but it is only where their individual character is most irregular, and education and laws at their worst. In general, it is nothing but pure self-will, and belongs to the two extremes of the community, — the most powerful, whose passions have been indulged; and the poorest, whose passions have never been instructed. True energy manifests itself, not in violence, but in strength and intensity; and intensity is by its nature discerning, and not to be surpassed in quietness, where quietness is becoming. Besides, in the age we are writing of, there was as much refinement in love-matters with some as there was outrage and brutality with others. All the faculties of humanity, bad and good, may be said to have been making their way at that period, and trying for the mastery: and if, on the one hand, we are presented with horrible spectacles of brute passion, tyranny, and revenge; on the other we find philosophy, and even divinity, refining upon the sentiment of love, and emulating the most beautiful subtleties of Plato in rendering it a thing angelical.

Reader. You have convinced me, sir: pray, let us proceed.

Author. Your *us*, madam, is flattering. I fancy we are beholding the two lovers in company. We are like Don Cleofas and his ghostly friend, in the "Devil on Two Sticks," when they saw into the people's houses: I, of course, the Devil; and you the young student, only feminine, — Donna Cleofasia, studying humanity.

Reader. Well, sir, as you please: only let us proceed.

Author. Madam, your sentiments are engaging to the last degree: so I proceed with pleasure.

We left our two lovers, madam, standing in Gossip Veronica's bed-chamber, one at the window, the other at a little distance. They remained in this situation about the same space of time in which we have been talking. Oh! how impossible it is to present to ourselves two grave and happy lovers trembling with the approach of their mutual confessions, and not feel a graver and happier sensation than levity resume its place in one's thoughts!

Ippolito went up to Dianora. She was still looking out of the window, her eyes fixed upon the blue mountains in the distance, but conscious of nothing outside the room. She had a light green and gold net on her head, which enclosed her luxuriant hair without violence, and seemed as if it took it up that he might admire the white neck underneath. She felt his breath upon it; and, beginning to expect that his lips would follow, raised her hands to her head, as if the net required adjusting. This movement, while it disconcerted him, presented her waist in a point of view so impossible not to touch, that, taking it gently in both his hands, he pressed one at the same time upon her heart, and said, "It will forgive me, even for doing this." He had reason to say so; for he felt it beat against his fingers, as if it leaped. Dianora, blushing and confused, though feeling abundantly happy, made another movement with her hands, as if to remove his own ; but he only detained them on either side. "Messer Ippolito," said Dianora, in a tone as if to remonstrate, though suffering herself to remain a prisoner, "I fear you must think me"—"No, no," interrupted Ippolito: "you can fear nothing that I think, or that I do. It is I that have to fear your lovely and fearful beauty, which has been ever at the side of my sick-bed, and, I thought, looked angrily upon me, —upon me alone of the whole world."—"They told me you had been ill," said Dianora in a very gentle tone; "and my aunt perhaps knew that I—thought that I—have you been very ill?" And, without thinking, she drew her left hand from under his, and placed it upon it. "Very," answered Ippolito: "do not I look so?" And, saying this, he raised his other hand, and, venturing to put it round to the left side of her little dimpled chin, turned her face towards him. Dianora did not think he appeared so ill, by a good deal, as he did in the church: but there was enough in his face, ill or well, to make her eyesight swim as she looked at him; and the next moment her head was upon his shoulder, and his lips descended, welcome, upon hers.

There was a practice in those times, generated, like other involuntary struggles against wrong, by the absurdities in authority, of resorting to marriages, or rather plightings of troth, made in secret and in the eye of Heaven. It was a custom liable to great abuse, as all secrecies are; but the harm of it, as usual, fell chiefly on the poor, or where the condition of the parties was unequal. Where the families were powerful, and on an equality, the hazard of violating the engagement was, for obvious reasons, very great, and seldom encountered; the lovers either foregoing their claims on each other upon better acquaintance, or adhering to their engagement the closer for the same reason, or keeping it at the expense of one or the other's repentance for fear of the consequences. The troth of Ippolito and Dianora was indeed a troth. They plighted it on their knees, before a picture of the Virgin and Child, in Veronica's bedroom, and over a mass-book which lay open upon a chair. Ippolito then, for the pleasure of revenging himself on the pangs he suffered when Dianora knelt with him before, took up the mass-book, and held it before her, as she had held it before him, and looked her entreatingly in the face; and Dianora took and held it with him as before, trembling as then, but with a perfect pleasure; and Ippolito kissed her twice and thrice out of a sweet revenge. [We find we are in the habit of using a great number of *ands* on these occasions. We do not affect it, though we are conscious of it. It is partly, we believe, owing to our recollections of the good faith and simplicity in the old romances, and partly to a certain sense of luxury and continuance which these *ands* help to link together. It is the fault of "the accursed critical spirit," which is the bane of these times, that we are obliged to be conscious of the matter at all. But we cannot help not having been born six hundred years ago, and are obliged to be base and *reviewatory* like the rest. To affect not to be conscious of the critical in these times, would itself be a departure from what is natural; but we notice the necessity only to express our hatred of it, and hereby present the critics (ourselves included, as far as we belong to them) with our hearty discommendations.]

The thoughtless old ladies, Donna Lucrezia and the other (for old age is not always the most considerate thing in the world, especially the old age of one's aunts and gossips), had now returned into the room where they left the two lovers; but not before Dianora had consented to receive her bridegroom in her own apartment at home, that same night, by means of that other old good-natured go-between, yclept a ladder of ropes. The rest of the afternoon was spent, according to laudable custom, in joining in the diversions of the peasantry. They sung, they danced, they ate the grapes that hung over their heads, they gave and took jokes and flowers, they flaunted with all their colors in the sun, they feasted with all their might under the trees. You could not say which looked the ripest and merriest, the fruit or their brown faces. In Tuscany, they have had from time immemorial little rustic songs or stanzas that turn upon flowers. One of these, innocently addressed to Dianora by way of farewell, put her much out of countenance. "Voi siete un bel fiore," sung a peasant girl, after kissing her hand:—

"You are a lovely flower. What flower? The flower
That shuts with the dark hour:
Would that to keep you awake were in my power!"

Ippolito went singing it all the way home, and ran up against a hundred people.

Ippolito had noticed a ladder of ropes which was used in his father's house for some domestic purposes.

To say the truth, it was an old servant, and had formerly been much in request for the purpose to which it was now about to be turned, by the old gentleman himself. He was indeed a person of a truly orthodox description, having been much given to intrigue in his younger days; being consigned over to avarice in his older, and exhibiting great submission to every thing established, always. Accordingly, he was considered as a personage equally respectable for his virtues, as important from his rank and connections; and, if hundreds of ladders could have risen up in judgment against him, they would only have been considered as what are called in England "wild oats,"—wild ladders, which it was natural for every gentleman to plant.

Ippolito's character, however, being more principled, his privileges were not the same; and, on every account, he was obliged to take great care. He waited with impatience till midnight, and then, letting himself out of his window, and taking the ropes under his cloak, made the best of his way to a little dark lane which bordered the house of the Bardi. One of the windows of Dianora's chamber looked into the lane, the others into the garden. The house stood in a remote part of the city. Ippolito listened to the diminishing sound of the guitars and revellers in the distance, and was proceeding to inform Dianora of his arrival by throwing up some pebbles, when he heard a noise coming. It was some young men taking a circuit of the more solitary streets, to purify them, as they said, from sobriety. Ippolito slunk into a corner. He was afraid, as the sound opened upon his ears, that they would turn down the lane; but the hubbub passed on. He stepped forth from his corner, and again retreated. Two young men, loiterers behind the rest, disputed whether they should go down the lane. One, who seemed intoxicated, swore he would serenade "the little foe," as he called her, if it was only to vex the old one, and "bring him out with his cursed long sword."—"And a lecture twice as long," said the other. "Ah! there you have me," quoth the musician. "His sword is—a sword: but his lecture's the Devil; reaches the other side of the river; never stops till it strikes one sleepy. But I must serenade."—"No, no," returned his friend: "remember what the grand prior said, and don't let us commit ourselves in a pretty brawl. We'll have it out of their hearts some day." Ippolito shuddered to hear such words, even from one of his own party. "Don't tell me," said the pertinacious, drunken man: "I remember what the grand prior said. He said, I must serenade: no, he didn't say I must serenade; but *I* say it. The grand prior said, says he,—I remember it as if it was yesterday,—he said, 'Gentlemen,' said he, 'there are three good things in the world,—love, music, and fighting:' and then he said a cursed number of other things by no means good; and all to prove, philosophically, you rogue! that love was good, and music was good, and fighting was good, philosophically, and in a cursed number of paragraphs. So I must serenade."—"False logic, Vanni!" cried the other: "so come along, or we shall have the enemy upon us in a heap; for I hear another party coming, and I am sure they are none of ours."—"Good again," said the musician; "love and fighting, my boy, and music: so I'll have my song before they come up." And the fellow began roaring out one of the most indecent songs he could think of, which made our lover ready to start forth, and dash the guitar in his face; but he repressed himself. In a minute, he heard the other party come up. A clashing of swords ensued; and, to his great relief, the drunkard and his companion were driven on. In a minute or two, all was silent. Ippolito gave the signal, — it was acknowledged; the rope was fixed; and the lover was about to ascend, when he was startled with a strange diminutive face, smiling at him over a light. His next sensation was to smile at the state of his own nerves; for it was but a few minutes before that he was regretting he could not put out a lantern that stood burning under a little image of the Virgin. He crossed himself, offered up a prayer for the success of his true love, and again proceeded to mount the ladder. Just as his hand reached the window, he thought he heard other steps. He looked down towards the street. Two figures evidently stood at the corner of the lane. He would have concluded them to be the two men returned, but for their profound silence. At last, one of them said out loud, "I am certain I saw a shadow of somebody by the lantern; and now you find we have not come back for nothing. Who's there?" added he, coming at the same time down the lane with his companion. Ippolito descended rapidly, intending to hide his face as much as possible in his hood, and escape by dint of fighting; but his foot slipped in the ropes, and he was, at the same instant, seized by the strangers. The instinct of a lover, who, above all things in the world, cared for his mistress's reputation, supplied our hero with an artifice as quick as lightning. "They are all safe," said he, affecting to tremble with a cowardly terror: "I have not touched one of them." "One of what?" said the others: "what are all safe?" "The jewels," replied Ippolito: "let me go for the love of God; and it shall be my last offence, as it was my first. Besides, I meant to restore them."—"Restore them!" cried the first spokesman: "a pretty jest, truly. This must be some gentleman gambler by his fine would-be conscience; and by this light we will see who he is, if it is only for your sake, Filippo; eh?" For his companion was a pretty notorious gambler himself, and Ippolito had kept cringing in the dark. "Curse it!" said Filippo, "never mind the fellow: he is not worth our while in these stirring times, though I warrant he has cheated me often enough." To say the truth, Messer Filippo was not a little afraid that the thief would turn out to be some inexperienced desperado whom he had cheated himself, and perhaps driven to this very crime: but his companion was resolute; and Ippolito, finding it impossible to avoid his fate, came forward into the light. "By all the saints in the calendar!" exclaimed the enemy, "a Buondelmonte! and no less a Buondelmonte than the worthy and very magnificent Messer Ippolito Buondelmonte! Messer Ippolito, I kiss your hands: I am very much your humble servant and thief-taker. By my faith, this will be fine news for to-morrow."

To-morrow was indeed a heavy day to all the Buondelmonti; and as merry a one to all the Bardi, except poor Dianora. She knew not what had prevented

Ippolito from finishing his ascent up the ladder: some interruption it must have been; but of what nature she could not determine, nor why he had not resumed his endeavors. It could have been nothing common. Was he known? Was *she* known? Was it all known? And the poor girl tormented herself with a thousand fears. Madonna Lucrezia hastened to her, the first thing in the morning, with a full, true, and particular account. Ippolito de' Buondelmonti had been seized, in coming down a rope-ladder from one of the front windows of the house, with a great drawn sword in one hand, and a box of jewels in the other. Dianora saw the whole truth in a moment; and, from excess of sorrow, gratitude, and love, fainted away. Madonna Lucrezia guessed the truth too, but was almost afraid to confess it to her own mind, much more to speak of it aloud; and had not the news, and the bustle, and her niece's fainting, furnished her with something to do, she could have fainted herself very heartily, out of pure consternation. Gossip Veronica was in a worse condition when the news reached her; and Ippolito's mother, who guessed but too truly as well as the others, was seized with an illness, which, joining with the natural weakness of her constitution, threw her into a stupor, and prevented her from attending to any thing. The next step of Madonna Lucrezia, after seeing Dianora out of her fainting fit, and giving the household to understand that the story of the robber had alarmed her, was to go to Gossip Veronica, and concert measures of concealment. The two women wept very sincerely for the poor youth, and admired his heroism in saving his mistress's honor; but, with all their good-nature, they agreed that he was quite in the right, and that it would be but just to his magnanimity, and to their poor dear Dianora, to keep the secret as closely. Madonna Lucrezia then returned home, to be near Dianora, and help to baffle inquiry; while Gossip Veronica kept close in-doors, too ill to see visitors, and alternately praying to the saint her namesake, and taking reasonable draughts of Montepulciano.

In those days, there were too many wild young men of desperate fortunes to render Ippolito's confession improbable. Besides, he had been observed of late to be always without money: reports of his being addicted to gambling had arisen; and his father was avaricious. Lastly, his groaning in the church was remembered, under pretence of pity; and the magistrate (who was of the hostile party) concluded, with much sorrow, that he must have more sins to answer for than they knew of, which, in so young a man, was deplorable. The old gentleman had too much reason to know, that, in older persons, it would have been nothing remarkable.

Ippolito, with a grief of heart which only served to confirm the by-standers in their sense of his guilt, waited in expectation of his sentence. He thought it would be banishment, and was casting in his mind how he could hope some day or other to get a sight of his mistress, when the word "death" fell on him like a thunderbolt. The origin of a sentence so severe was but too plain to everybody: but the Bardi were uppermost that day; and the city, exhausted by some late party excesses, had but too much need of repose.

Still it was thought a dangerous trial of the public pulse. The pity felt for the tender age of Ippolito was increased by the anguish which he found himself unable to repress. "Good God!" cried he, "must I die so young? And must I never see — must I never see the light again, and Florence, and my dear friends?" And he fell into almost abject entreaties to be spared; for he thought of Dianora. But the by-standers fancied that he was merely afraid of death; and, by the help of suggestions from the Bardi partisans, their pity almost turned into contempt. He prostrated himself at the magistrate's feet; he kissed his knees; he disgusted his own father; till, finding every thing against him, and smitten at once with a sense of his cowardly appearance, and the necessity of keeping his mistress's honor inviolable, he declared his readiness to die like a man; and, at the same time, stood wringing his hands, and weeping like an infant. He was sentenced to die next day.

The day came. The hour came. The Standard of Justice was hoisted before the door of the tribunal; and the trumpet blew through the city, announcing the death of a criminal. Dianora, to whom the news had been gradually broken, heard it in her chamber, and would have burst forth, and proclaimed the secret, but for Madonna Lucrezia, who spoke of her father and mother and all the Bardi, and the inutility of attempting to save one of the opposite faction, and the dreadful consequences to *every*-body if the secret were betrayed. Dianora heard little about everybody; but the habit of respecting her father and mother, and dreading their reproaches, kept her, moment after moment, from doing any thing but listen, and look pale; and, in the mean time, the procession began moving towards the scaffold.

Ippolito issued forth from the prison, looking more like a young martyr than a criminal. He was now perfectly quiet, and a sort of unnatural glow had risen into his cheeks, the result of the enthusiasm and conscious self-sacrifice into which he had worked himself during the night. He had only prayed, as a last favor, that he might be taken through the street in which the house of the Bardi stood: for he had lived, he said, as everybody knew, in great hostility with that family; and he now felt none any longer, and wished to bless the house as he passed it. The magistrate, for more reasons than one, had no objection: the old confessor, with tears in his eyes, said that the dear boy would still be an honor to his family, as surely as he would be a saint in heaven; and the procession moved on. The main feeling of the crowd, as usual, was that of curiosity; but there were few, indeed, in whom it was not mixed with pity: and many females found the sight so intolerable, that they were seen coming away down the streets, weeping bitterly, and unable to answer the questions of those they met.

The procession now began to pass the house of the Bardi. Ippolito's face, for an instant, turned of a chalky whiteness, and then resumed its color. His lips trembled, his eyes filled with tears; and thinking his mistress might possibly be at the window, taking a last look of the lover that died for her, he bowed his head gently, at the same time forcing a smile, which glittered through his watery eyes. At that instant, the trumpet blew its dreary blast for the second time. Dianora had already risen on her couch, listening, and asking what noise it was that approached. Her aunt endeavored to quiet her with excuses: but this last noise aroused her beyond control; and the good old lady, forgetting herself in the condition of the two lovers, no longer attempted to stop her. "Go," said she, "in God's name, my child; and Heaven be with you!"

Dianora, her hair streaming, her eye without a tear, her cheek on fire, burst, to the astonishment of her kindred, into the room where they were all standing. She tore them aside from one of the windows with a preternatural strength; and, stretching forth her head and hands, like one inspired, cried out, "Stop, stop! it is my Ippolito! my husband!" And, so saying, she actually made a movement as if she would have stepped to him out of the window; for every thing but his image faded from her eyes. A movement of confusion took place among the multitude. Ippolito stood rapt on the sudden, trembling, weeping, and stretching his hands towards the window, as if praying to his guardian angel. The kinsmen would have prevented her from doing any thing further; but, as if all the gentleness of her character was gone, she broke from them with violence and contempt, and, rushing down stairs into the street, exclaimed, in a frantic manner, "People! dear God! countrymen! I am a Bardi; he is a Buondelmonte: he loved me; and that is the whole crime!" and, at these last words, they were locked in each other's arms.

The populace now broke through all restraint.

They stopped the procession; they bore Ippolito back again to the seat of the magistracy, carrying Dianora with him; they described in a peremptory manner the mistake; they sent for the heads of the two houses; they made them swear a treaty of peace, amity, and unity; and, in half an hour after the lover had been on the road to his death, he set out upon it again, the acknowledged bridegroom of the beautiful creature by his side.

Never was such a sudden revulsion of feeling given to a whole city. The women who had retreated in anguish came back the gayest of the gay. Everybody plucked all the myrtles they could find, to put into the hands of those who made the former procession, and who now formed a singular one for a bridal: but all the young women fell in with their white veils; and, instead of the funeral dirge, a song of thanksgiving was chanted. The very excess of their sensations enabled the two lovers to hold up. Ippolito's cheeks, which seemed to have fallen away in one night, appeared to have plumped out again faster; and if he was now pale, instead of high-colored, the paleness of Dianora had given way to radiant blushes which made up for it. He looked as he ought, — like the person saved; she, like the angelic savior.

Thus the two lovers passed on, as if in a dream tumultuous but delightful. Neither of them looked on the other; they gazed hither and thither on the crowd, as if in answer to the blessings that poured upon them: but their hands were locked fast, and they went like one soul in a divided body.

RHYME AND REASON;

Or, a New Proposal to the Public respecting Poetry in Ordinary.

 FRIEND of ours the other day, taking up the miscellaneous poems of Tasso, read the titlepage into English as follows, — "The Rhymes of the Lord Twisted Yew, Amorous, Bosky, and Maritime."* The Italians exhibit a modesty worthy of imitation in calling their miscellaneous poems "rhymes." Twisted Yew himself, with all his genius, has put forth an abundance of these terminating blossoms, without any fruit behind them; and his countrymen of the present day do not scruple to confess, that their living poetry consists of little else. The French have a game at verses, called Rhymed Ends (*Bouts Rimés*), which they practise a great deal more than they are aware; and the English, though they are a more poetical people, and lay claim to the character of a less vain one, practise the same game to a very uncandid extent, without so much as allowing that the title is applicable to any part of it.

Yet how many "poems" are there among all these nations, of which we require no more than the rhymes to be acquainted with the whole of them?

* "Rime del Signor Torquato Tasso, Amorose, Boschereccie, Marittime," &c.

You know what the rogues have done by the ends they come to. For instance, what more is necessary to inform us of all which the following gentleman has for sale, than the bell which he tinkles at the end of his cry? We are as sure of him as of the muffin-man.

A LOVE-SONG.

Grove,	Heart,	Kiss,
Night,	Prove,	Blest,
Rove,	Impart,	Bliss,
Delight.	Love.	Rest.

Was there ever peroration more eloquent?—ever a series of catastrophes more explanatory of their previous history? Did any Chinese gentleman ever show the amount of his breeding and accomplishments more completely by the nails which he carries at his fingers' ends?

The Italian Rimatori are equally comprehensive. We no sooner see the majority of their rhymes, than we long to save the modesty of their general pretensions so much trouble in making out their case. Their *cores* and *amores* are not to be disputed. Cursed is he that does not put implicit reliance upon their *fedeltà!*—that makes inquisition why the possessor *più superbo va.* They may take the oaths and their seat at once. For example:—

Ben mio	Fuggito
Oh Dio	Rapito
Per te.	Da me.

And again:—

Amata	Furore
Sdegnata	Dolore
Turbata	Non so.
Irata	

With —

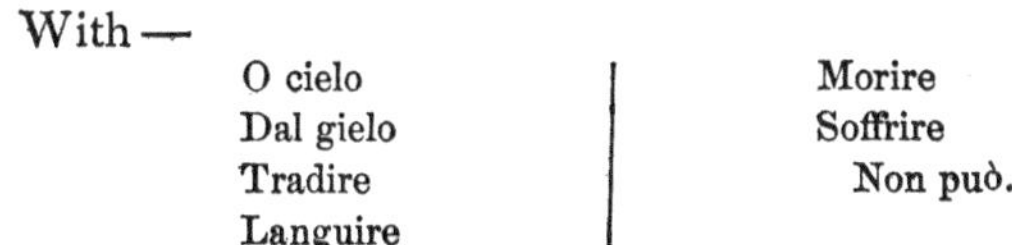

O cielo
Dal gielo
Tradire
Languire
Morire
Soffrire
Non può.

Where is the dull and inordinate person that would require these rhymes to be filled up? If they are brief as the love of which they complain, are they not pregnant in conclusions, full of a world of things that have passed, infinitely retrospective, embracing, and enough? If not "vast," are they not "voluminous"?

It is doubtless an instinct of this kind that has made so many modern Italian poets intersperse their lyrics with those frequent single words, which are at once line and rhyme, and which some of our countrymen have in vain endeavored to naturalize in the English opera. Not that they want the same pregnancy in our language, but because they are neither so abundant nor so musical; and, besides, there is something in the rest of our verses, however commonplace, which seems to be laughing at the incursion of these vivacious strangers, as if it were a hop suddenly got up, and unseasonably. We do not naturally take to any thing so abrupt and saltatory.

This objection, however, does not apply to the proposal we are about to make. Our rhymers *must* rhyme; and as there is a great difference between single words thus mingled with longer verses, and the same rhymes in their proper places, it has struck us that a world of time and paper might be saved to the ingenious *rimatore*, whether Italian or English, by foregoing at once all the superfluous part of his verses,

— that is to say, all the rest of them; and confining himself entirely to these very sufficing terminations. We subjoin some specimens in the various kinds of poetry; and inform the intelligent bookseller, that we are willing to treat with him for any quantity at a penny a hundred: —

A PASTORAL.

Dawn	Each	Fair	Me	Ray
Plains	Spoke	Mine	Too	Heat
Lawn	Beech	Hair	Free	Play
Swains.	Yoke.	Divine.	Woo.	Sweet.
Tune	Fields	Shades	Adieu	Farewell
Lays	Bowers	Darts	Flocks	Cows
Moon	Yields	Maids	Renew	Dell
Gaze.	Flowers.	Hearts.	Rocks.	Boughs.

Here, without any more ado, we have the whole history of a couple of successful rural lovers comparing notes. They issue forth in the morning; fall into the proper place and dialogue; record the charms and kindness of their respective mistresses; do justice at the same time to the fields and shades; and conclude by telling their flocks to wait, as usual, while they renew their addresses under the boughs. How easily is all this gathered from the rhymes! and how worse than useless would it be in two persons, who have such interesting avocations, to waste their precious time and the reader's in a heap of prefatory remarks, falsely called verses!

Of love-songs we have already had specimens; and, by the by, we did not think it necessary to give any French examples of our involuntary predecessors in this species of writing. The *yeux* and *dangereux*, *moi* and *foi*, *charmes* and *larmes*, are too well known as well as too numerous to mention. We proceed to lay before the reader a prologue; which, if spoken by a pretty actress, with a due sprinkling of nods and becks, and a judicious management of the pauses, would have an effect equally novel and triumphant. The reader is aware that a prologue is generally made up of some observations on the drama in general, followed by an appeal in favor of the new one, some compliments to the nation, and a regular climax in honor of the persons appealed to. We scarcely need observe, that the rhymes should be read slowly, in order to give effect to the truly understood remarks in the intervals.

PROLOGUE.

Age	Fashion	Applause
Stage	British nation.	Virtue's cause.
Mind		
Mankind	Young	Trust
Face	Tongue	Just
Trace	Bard	Fear
Sigh	Reward	Here
Tragedy	Hiss	Stands
Scene	Miss	Hands
Spleen	Dare	True
Pit	British fair.	You.
Wit.		

Here we have some respectable observations on the advantages of the drama in every age, on the wideness of its survey, the different natures of tragedy and comedy, the vicissitudes of fashion, and the permanent greatness of the British Empire. Then the young bard, new to the dramatic art, is introduced. He disclaims all hope of reward for any merit of his own, except that which is founded on a proper sense of the delicacy and beauty of his fair auditors, and his zeal in the cause of virtue. To this, at all events, he is sure his critics will be just; and though he cannot help feeling a certain timidity, standing where he does, yet upon the whole, as becomes an Englishman, he is perfectly willing to abide by the decision of his countrymen's hands, hoping that he shall be found—

"To sense, if not to genius, true;
And trusts his cause to virtue, and—to YOU."

Should the reader, before he comes to this explication of the prologue, have had any other ideas suggested by it, we will undertake to say, that they will, at all events, be found to have a wonderful general similitude; and it is to be observed, that this very flexibility of adaptation is one of the happiest and most useful results of our proposed system of poetry. It comprehends all the possible commonplaces in vogue; and it also leaves to the ingenious reader something to fill up; which is a compliment that has always been held due to him by the best authorities.

The next specimen is what, in a more superfluous condition of metre, would have been entitled "*Lines* on Time." It is much in that genteel didactic taste, which is at once thinking and non-thinking; and has a certain neat and elderly dislike of innovation in it, greatly to the comfort of the seniors who adorn the circles.

ON TIME.

Time
Sublime
Fraught
Thought
Power
Devour
Rust
Dust
Glass
Pass
Wings
Kings.

Child
Beguiled
Boy
Joy
Man
Span
Sire
Expire.

So
Go.

Race
Trace
All
Ball
Pride
Deride
Aim
Same
Undo
New.

Hold
Old
Sure
Endure
Death
Breath
Forgiven
Heaven.

We ask any impartial reader, whether he could possibly want a more sufficing account of the progress of this author's piece of reasoning upon Time. There is, first, the address to the hoary god, with all his emblems and consequence about him, the scythe excepted; that being an edge-tool to rhymers, which they judiciously keep inside the verse, as in a sheath. And then we are carried through all the stages of human existence, the caducity of which the writer applies to the world at large, impressing upon us the inutility of hope and exertion, and suggesting, of course, the propriety of thinking just as he does upon all subjects, political and moral, past, present, and to come.

1822.

VICISSITUDES OF A LECTURE;

OR,

Public Elegance and Private Non-Particularity.

OOR NED POUNCHY! He is no longer alive; otherwise we should not risk the wounding of his good-natured eyes by these pages. Neither was he ever known enough to the many to undergo the hazard of their now digging him up again; and, finally, we have obscured the illustrious obscurity of his name by an *alias.* We may, therefore, without offence, resuscitate a passage in his life for the amusement of those critical readers whom it was his highest ambition to gratify.

Ned Pounchy had long been seized with a passionate desire to give a lecture,—his favorite mode of literary intercourse,—and on Shakespeare and Milton, his favorite poets. Accordingly, after a series of blissful preparations and half-threatening obstacles, which only perfected the pleasure of the result, he found himself one evening at the upper end of a great room in a certain tavern, standing with book in hand, and in most consummate black satin small-clothes and silk stockings (the former very crinkled and scholarly), with a great screen at his back, and an expectant set of beholders in front of him, to whom he had undertaken to set forth the merits of a scene or two in the

"Tempest," and to recite Milton's charming poems, "Allegro" and "Penseroso."

Now, our friend Pounchy, or rather our friend's friend (for we had no particular knowledge of him, except on this occasion), was a somewhat stout and short man, like many an eminent individual before and since, of some forty or five and forty years of age; and if, unlike them, he seemed to think his person qualified to compete with his intellectual attractions, and to require only "a fair stage and no favor," yet his genial disposition did (there can be no doubt of it) instinctively suggest to itself, that the favor would be granted him; and, in fact, he appeared so *coscy* and comfortable, and after-dinner-like, in the very midst of a certain elevation of neckcloth and powdered head, that it was impossible not to sympathize with his satisfaction, and be prepared to relish whatever taste he should be pleased to give us of his critical nicety. He had no rostrum or desk before him. All in that respect was open and above-board; undisguised as his good faith; and, as he walked to and fro, his shoes creaked a little.

Suddenly, after a brief but serious conference with some head that emerged from behind the screen, and returning towards us with a *hum* and *haw*, intermingled with applications of white handkerchief, he opened upon his audience with a brief introduction to the first scene of the "Tempest." His tones were of an importance commensurate with the fame of his author; and none of the homely seamanship in the text beguiled him, for an instant, out of a due respect for it. Not that he omitted to expatiate on the extreme naturalness of the scene: that was a point which Ned evidently regarded as one of the most serious objects of his duty to impress upon us. He could not have been more emphatic, or given us greater time to deliberate on what we heard, had he recited the soliloquy in "Hamlet." Thus, instead of those excellent but too uncritical imitators of seamen, Mr. T. P. Cooke, Mr. Smith, and others, conceive the following exordium of the play set forth in its utmost solemnity of articulation by the mouth of Mr. Ward or Mr. Barrymore; accompanied furthermore by a mention, at once particular and careless, and singularly incorporating itself with the text, of the *name* of the party speaking; which, if you reflect upon it, was a very great nicety, and showed the lecturer's just sense of all which he could be expected to combine in his delivery, as holding the double office of reader and performer. Repeat, for instance, out loud, and very slowly, the following words; and the sound of your voice will enable you the better to appreciate our critic's delicacy: —

Enter a SHIPMASTER *and a* BOATSWAIN.
Master Boatswain —

(which you are to read as if he was speaking of a young gentleman of the name of Boatswain, son of John Boatswain, Esq., — "Master Boatswain.")

Boatswain Here, master; what — cheer —

("What — cheer," very slow and pompous.)

Master Good

(here another young gentleman, son of Thomas Good, Esquire, — young "Master Good.")

— speak — to — the mariner — fall — to it — yarely, or we run ourselves — aground — Bestir — bestir.

(Bestir, bestir, very wide apart, and all pompous.)

Exit — master. Enter — Mariners.
Boatswain Heigh —

(Here it seems to transpire that the boatswain's name is Heigh or Hay, — "Boatswain Hay.")

Boatswain Heigh — my heart — cheerly — cheerly — my heart; — yare — yare — Take in — the topsail

(all observe, as if he were reading some mighty text in a pulpit.)

— take in — the topsail — tend — to the master's — whistle —

And so he went on, amidst the deep and admiring silence of the spectators, whose shoulders you might observe, here and there, gradually begin shaking, out of some irrepressible emotion. A wag, who has a lively but confused recollection of the scene, insists that there was a passage in the dialogue, which upon examination we cannot find, but which he delights to repeat as having been thus delivered, — very slow and pompous, yet with the remarkable absence of stops between the names and words of the speakers, and all in a level tone: —

First Boatswain Hip — hollo-a
Second Boatswain Hollo-a —hip.

But this is manifestly a figment, superinduced upon a strongly excited fancy.

Of the rest of this scene from the "Tempest," singularly enough, we have no sort of recollection. Whether this forgetfulness be owing to some unremembered stoppage on the part of the reciter, or to the criticisms of the friends about us, or some uproarious sympathy analogous to the tumult on board ship, we cannot say; but the thing has clean gone out of our memory. All we can call to mind is a little thin old gentleman, probably a friend of the lecturer's, who kept going about among the benches, smiling, and apparently asking the ladies how they liked it; and exhibiting a hand laden with rings.

But now came the "Allegro." Our memory serves us very well on this point, for reasons which will be obvious: —

"HENCE, — *loathed* — MEL-ancholy"

began Ned, in the most vehement, but at the same time dignified manner you can conceive, — absolutely startling us, — his mouth thrust out, his eye fierce, his right arm extended at full length, tossing his head, and then *pointing;* in short, telling Melancholy to go to the greatest possible distance, and as if showing her whereabouts it was.

"Hence — loathed — Melancholy —
Of Cerberus — 'and — BLACK-est — midnight born"

("Blackest" excessively black on the first syllable)

"In — Stygian — cave — forlorn —
Midst — horrid shapes — and sights — and shrieks — unholy" —

"unholy" with an immense emphasis on the *o*. And so he went on till he came to the words "Come and trip it;" for though the feeling in the poet's mind changes wonderfully from the repelling to the engaging, in that alteration of the measure, where he says, "But come, thou goddess fair and free," yet Ned seemed to think, that, as both the passages were equally good, it was his duty to regard their merits with impartiality, and not risk the appreciation of the cheerfuller lines by any levity of approach. His "Come — thou Goddess — fair — and free," was therefore delivered in precisely the same tones as the rest, — immeasurably grave, earnest, and emphatical, and as if every syllable he uttered was commissioned to maintain the united dignity of the poetical and reciting characters.

But now comes, not only the cheerfulness, but the catastrophe. "Great wits have short memories," said somebody; probably because he had one himself. Ned, however, was at all events *a brother* instance; for after getting through the "Graces" and "Aurora," and the "fresh-blown roses," and "quips and cranks," &c., with the most extraordinary solemnity (and it was no great distance to get), he stuck fast at the very spot where he was bound to proceed in his happiest manner; to wit, upon the line, —

> "Come and trip it, as you go."

He remembered "Come and trip it;" but he could not, for the life of him, conjure up "as you go."

The head behind the screen was now heard, *prompting*, —

> "Come and trip it, as you go."

But Ned, it turned out, was unfortunately deaf, and the words were lost upon him.

> "Come and trip it, *as you go*,"

said the voice, still in a whisper, but with greater emphasis.

In vain. Ned bent his head again to catch the words, and again they were repeated with emphasis still greater, but always in a whisper, —

"Come and trip it, AS YOU GO."

In vain again. Once more Ned bent his head, with all its painstaking and powder; and again the words were sent forth, in a sort of whisper in a rage, —

"Come and trip it, AS YOU GO."

"Good God!" the whisper seemed to say, "will you *never* hear me?"

The reader must imagine the audience all this time hearing what the lecturer could not hear, as plainly as their own words, and ready to burst.

At length, he does catch the words; and, with an irresistible air of hilarity and self-satisfaction (as if the little obstacle were removed from between him and his triumphs), resumes his stately way: —

"Come — and trip it — as you go —
On the *light*"

("light" very heavy)

"fantastic-toe;"

("fantastic," imperious;)

"And — in thy — right hand — lead — with thee
The mountain — nymph — sweet — Liberty
And — if I — give thee — honor — due —
Mirth — admit me — of — *thy* crew —
To live — with her — and live — with thee
In — un — reproved — pleasures — free."

Alas! while in the act of arriving at these pleasures, and little thinking that he was about to disclose what they were, he unfortunately kept stepping backwarder and backwarder, till in a moment he bolted against the screen, and DOWN IT WENT! exhibiting, — besides the enraged individual to whom the voice belonged, — what do you think?

A bottle of wine and some cakes?

No.

A few oranges, perhaps?

By no means.

A sandwich?

Not in the least.

What then?

A pot of ale, and some bread and cheese.

There was no harm in it. Geniuses have made many a hearty meal upon bread and cheese, and been glad that they could get it: only, somehow, the highly poetical dignity of the recitation, the immense idealism of the lecturer, and the aristocracy of the satin small-clothes, had not prepared the spectators for so unsophisticate a refreshment; and they were glad to pretend an outcry of alarm and sympathy, in order to drown what they could of the otherwise inextinguishable laughter which shook the place.

What followed we totally forget, perhaps because we came away; but never shall we forget thee, and thy publicities and retirements, honest Ned Pounchy.

THE FORTUNES OF GENIUS.

IN the "Atlas," the other day, was an article, under the above title, the following passages of which induce us to make some remarks upon them. We regret we cannot copy the whole,— it is so well written, and shows such a relish of pleasure, and sympathy with pain. But our limits forbid.

"An acquaintance," says the writer, "with the biography of illustrious musicians proves that they reason incorrectly, and with a short sight, who externally talk of having the path of genius smoothed, and of setting it above circumstances; for the lives of eminent men of this class display the most admirable energies developed, and the most enthusiastic projects brought to bear, purely by the pressure of the very annoyances sought to be removed. Possession of the creative faculty presupposes a superiority to adverse circumstances and 'low-thoughted care;' and Goldsmith's poet, sitting in his garret, with a worsted stocking on his head,—

> 'Where the Red Lion, staring o'er the way,
> Invites each passing stranger *that can pay*,'—

in spite of bailiffs, writs, debts, duns, and milk-scores, the most horrible that even Hogarth imagined, was still a happy fellow. The individual Mr. Jones, seated before a delicate leg of lamb and a bottle of sherry, is an abstraction of the Mr. Jones who owes £284. 18*s*. 4*d*., and has, as the Dutchmen say, nix to pay. Satisfied that he would pay if he could, which is all that is necessary to place the *morale* of his character upon high ground, he leaves the affairs of the world to right themselves, and enjoys the everlasting day-rule of the imagination. [How well said is this!] So it was with Fielding, with Goldsmith, with Steele, and others honorable in literature, and so also with Handel, with Mozart, and Weber, in music; and it is one of the kindly recompenses of Nature, by which she contrives, on the whole, to adjust so equitably the good and the evil in this life, that, where injury to the individual arises from an excess of sympathy with the mass, that injury is commonly but lightly felt."

We were not aware that the trials of these musicians in pecuniary affairs were so great. The following information respecting Mozart is as startling as it is affecting: "Who thinks, when he looks over the six great operas of Mozart, and admires the Shakespearian knowledge of character, and the thoughtful discrimination appearing in every movement of them, that those master-pieces were produced amidst a tumult of arrests, and of the lowest annoyances that ever embroiled a life? Nay, it is even said that the family of Mozart at times wanted common necessaries. Adversity may have been a sharp thorn in the side of so gentle and enjoying a spirit as Mozart; but it would be affectation to deplore the circumstances that have put the musical world in possession of their most valued treasures." And here follows something awful respecting Handel, — an awful man. The hurried dashes and dative cases of the writer ("to his quarrel with Senesino," "to his madness and rage," "to his palsy") are like an agitato accompaniment to the facts. "The twenty or thirty folio volumes bearing the names of Handel's oratorios, which alone transmit his name to posterity, when we contemplate them in some well-ordered library, carry no thought of their having been produced after the composer had received the first signal of death in a stroke of palsy which disabled his arm. Ruin and disease, that fill the minds of men of more feeble powers with thoughts of the narrow coffin and the shroud, made Handel immortal. We owe the 'Messiah' and 'Israel in Egypt' to the composer's obstinate temper; to his quarrel with Senesino and the nobility; to his making rash engagements with singers that compelled him to withdraw his last guinea from the funds to satisfy them; to his madness and rage; to his palsy; to his proceeding to the vapor-baths of Aix-la-Chapelle, whence, with the purgation of his humors, reason and religion returned, and persuaded him that there was another style of music yet untried, more likely than operas to suit the grave character of the English. Then followed in rapid succession his immortal oratorios, — works in which the pure flame of his genius never shone more brightly, though produced at a late period of life, commenced after the attack of a threatening and fatal disorder, and ended in total blindness"

The question thus opened by the writer in the

"Atlas" is a great puzzle. We confess, that, in many respects, we take the same view of it as himself: for we reverence the past; we are inclined to think best of whatever has taken place, since it *has* taken place, — to conclude that good and evil somehow have adjusted themselves in the best manner; and we have such belief in the predominance of happy over unhappy feelings in the minds of men of genius, that we sometimes think they would have had an unfair portion of joy in their life, had their lot been less counterbalanced by difficulties, ill health, or whatsoever their troubles may have been.

But the question branches off into some others, which it may not be well for society to lose sight of; especially as, by the efforts which Providence incites them to make for the common good, it would seem, that, however necessary some portion of evil may always be for the proper relish of good, there may not always exist a necessity for it to an amount so large. One of these collateral questions we shall put.

Is it certain that the men of genius above mentioned would not have written as much, or as finely, under happier circumstances?

It is natural enough to conclude, that men so careless in worldly matters as Steele and Fielding, and with such a relish of the moment before them, when it contained the least drop of sweet, would perhaps have written *nothing at all.* Frightful supposition! And yet is the supposition likely, considering that very relish? Is it natural for people to be delighted, and hold their tongue? — to have fame at their command, and not command it? Or was it necessary for Handel to be so extremely pained before he could give us his sense of the passionate and the sublime? Was there not suffering enough for him, short of rage and madness? No firmament over his head, nor graves under his feet? Perhaps he yet needed his afflictions,—be it so, since they have happened; but might it not be perilous in future, seeing that we have become alive to such questions, to run the risk of steeling the hearts of people against the struggles of genius, if not for the latter's sake, yet for their own, and ultimately, by that process, for both? Whatsoever happens in the world without our being aware of it, we take to be one thing; what otherwise, to be another; and fate and consequence become modified accordingly. If the pain should remain the same after all, we still cannot be certain that it is necessary, however it will become us to hope so when it be past. The peril, meanwhile, is, that we shall be blunting our own feelings, and those of genius too.

Beaumont was of opinion that a man of genius could no more help putting his thoughts on paper, than a traveller in a burning desert can help drinking when he sees water.

> "I know full well, that no more than the man
> That travels through the burning deserts can,
> When he is beaten with the raging sun,
> Half smothered in the dust, have power to run
> From a cool river which himself doth find,
> Ere he bè slaked; no more can he whose mind
> Joys in the Muses hold from that delight,
> When Nature and his full thoughts bid him write."

Could Fielding have helped writing "Tom Jones" (the perfectest prose-fiction in the language) whether he had been in trouble or not? Could Steele have helped throwing his lighter, happier graces round the Muse of his friend Addison? Would Goldsmith's craving for reputation have allowed him to be silent with his pen (which was admirable), when he could not even refrain in company with his tongue? (which was nothing.) Or does the enjoying critic of the "Atlas," whose articles are like variations upon the musical beauties they criticise, dwelling upon them, and winding them in congenial tones round his heart, really think it would have been possible for Mozart to possess all that abundance of the soul of love and pleasure, and not cry aloud?—not burst forth and blossom like the peach-trees in spring?—not come pouring down from a hundred fountains of song into the surging sea of the orchestra, like the summer clouds from the mountains?

We grant that certain noble kinds of pain may be necessary to produce certain sublimities of composition, whether in musical or other writing; but need the composer be stimulated with the lowest and most humiliating cares to induce him to write at all, supposing him to be a real genius? Perhaps he would not write so much; but are we sure even of that, *supposing him to be put into a condition quite suitable to his nature?* Steele and Fielding and Mozart would not have written all the identical same works which they produced; but are we sure they would not have produced as many, or even better? Well-fed birds sing in cages; but the more philosophic of their jailers (strange people!) discern something, in the best of their imprisoned songs, inferior to their "wood-notes wild." Does the throstle on the bough, in order to pour gushes of melody from his heart, require a string to his leg, or a blink from some bailiff snake?

Walter Scott assuredly would not have written all his novels, had he not thought circumstances required it; but we should most likely have had his best. "Waverley" he wrote for love, when he did not dream that he should get a sixpence by it; and "Old Mortality" and "The Antiquary" soon followed the publication of that novel, — partly, no doubt, for profit, but much also by reason of love encouraged, and out of a love of the sense of power. These, his best, we should have had; and he would not have been killed by writing his worst. O Scotland! O England! O Europe! we might say, — for he belonged to all, — how could you suffer him to die?

And Burns — that other "glory and shame" of this island — he did not get (so to speak) a penny for his writings: for though, no doubt, he did get a good deal more, yet that was not the reason why he produced them; and numbers of his songs he gave away. Yes: he, the glorious ploughman and born gentleman, gave his songs away, free as the bird that he took for his crest. Now, Burns, if any man ever did, wrote for love, and not for money; yet his life was full of pecuniary distress.

And observe how many men of genius have written abundantly, who have had no sordid cares, — certainly none that writing settled for them, in a pecuniary sense. Chaucer is an illustrious instance; Spenser, another; Milton (though poor), another; Beaumont and Fletcher, Pope, Swift, Addison, Gibbon, Hume, Hooker, Sterne, Lamb, Wordsworth, Jeremy Taylor; in short, almost all our best, and *all* the Greek, Roman, and Italian men of genius (for nobody ever got *obolus* or *crazia* for his writings in the classical countries, ancient or modern). In Italy there is no payment of authors, any more than there was among the countrymen of Anacreon and Ovid; yet we have had, nevertheless, the Dantes, Petrarchs, and Ariostos. The Homers, to be sure, got their "feed," in the minstrel-times of Greece; but nobody supposes that those amazing rhapsodists would never have opened their mouths but for King Alcinous's pork-chops.

Then, among musicians, Haydn, we believe, was not distressed; nor the Corellis and Paesiellos. Gluck was rich. Nor have the best of the painters been poor, — the Raphaels, Michael Angelos, and Titians. On the contrary, with the exception of Rembrandt, those who have been best off in worldly affairs have generally been most abundant in pictorial produce, — sometimes, it is true, by help of the influx of wealth, as in Titian's case; but, at any rate, necessity was not the stimulant. Nor did patronage make them idle. No; because it was true, and lit on true men. The watered tree bore, because it possessed the seed. Do not Hummel, Spohr, and others, write, and write well, though made as comfortable as church-canons, in those little snug chapel-masterships of theirs, of which we are told so delightfully in the "Ramble among the Musicians in Germany"?

Often and often, we doubt not, — perhaps in all instances, — has inconsistency of position in men of genius been mistaken for idleness. It may be possible, in many cases, that temperament, or even too much thought, or other conflicting impulses, may produce something, in the appearance, which "the world calls idle;" but the true conflicting impulses, in perhaps all instances, have arisen from incompatibility of calls upon the attention. He who is forced to do incompatible or uncongenial things does them badly; or he sings, perhaps, at all events, and sings well: but sometimes he cannot sing at all; the wires of the cage of his necessity press too hard upon him; he wants breathing-room, nature, comfort; he sings at last, partly because he is forced, partly because it solaces him. But try the humane expedient of rescuing him from his worst cares, and see how he would sing then, — if not his most, yet surely his best: at least, so it appears to us.

Blessings, nevertheless, say we, with the genial philosopher of the "Atlas," upon the trouble and sorrow even of a sordid kind, if we could not have had certain men of genius without them; and blessings, at all events, upon the beauty into which they are converted, and the divine way which Nature has of making bitterness itself blossom and become medicinal. But let us take care how we sow opinions, unqualified, the fruits of which may intoxicate weak heads in after-times, — with careless assumption, if writers; with selfish references to Providence and necessity, if the arbiters of the fate of writers. Most writers of any ability are pretty well off in these times, and have a good patron in the public. But a time may come, (are we sure that it has in no case happened already?) when, by the very process of the abundance of writings, genius may want support; and let us not prepare our children's children to refuse it.

The absurdity of a tragedy, unfortunately, is not always an argument against its chances; but to show how very absurd this principle of leaving men of genius to their fate might become, if driven to all its consequences, let our contemporary, who understands and loves a joke run to seed (no man better), take the following scene between the future patron of a musical genius, and an emissary he has despatched to inquire into his circumstances: —

Patron. Well, Dick, and how did you find him? Will the composition of the new opera go on swimmingly?

Emissary. According to your grace, it will; for he is horribly off.

P. Good. What, in pressing want, eh? Can't afford to be idle?

E. If he did, he could not eat. The butcher would not trust him. The butcher says he is too honest a man to be trusted; he is such a child!

P. Excellent! just like your man of genius. And the butcher is a shrewd dog. But our new Mozart must not starve *quite:* we'll take care of that. Then he has finished, I presume, that capital scene of the feast, with that wonderful joyous dance? and that droll chorus, with the corpulent man in it?

E. He has; with a lawyer's letter on each side of him, and a face haggard with headache.

P. (*rubbing his hands*). Capital! We are sure then, you think, of the whole opera?

E. There is no doubt of it. His five children were looking out of the window, wondering whether the baker would come.

P. You rejoice me. We shall have a brilliant audience. And what did he say to you?

E. Oh! he smiled, as usual, and laughed, and said he wondered at his spirits, considering his headache; but I thought I almost saw the tears in his eyes as he said it.

P. A true genius! That's the way he gets his pathos, Dick. The man is all fire and feeling.

E. I suspect he would have been glad of a little more "fire" yesterday; for his servant told me he had no coals.

P. Bravo! Poor fellow! Oh! it's clear we shall do capitally. We must not let his fingers be cold, however, nor the baker fail his children.

E. Did your grace ever think of trying what a course of comfort would do for him?

P. A course of *what?* Ruin, Dick, ruin. I never did, of course; but who'd write if they could help it?

E. (*aside*). Not you, God knows; for it's as much as you can do to spell. Yet this is the great opera patron whom our "new Mozart" calls a "good kind of man, not over-imaginative"!

POETS' HOUSES.

PAPER in Mr. Disraeli's "Curiosities of Literature," upon "Literary Residences," is very amusing and curious: but it begins with a mistake in saying that "men of genius have usually been condemned to compose their finest works, which are usually their earliest ones, under the roof of a garret;" and the author seems to think that few have realized the sort of house they wished to live in. The combination of "genius and a garret" is an old joke, but little more. Genius has been often poor enough, but seldom so much so as to want what are looked upon as the decencies of life. In point of abode, in particular, we take it to have been generally lucky as to the fact, and not at all so grand in the desire as Mr. Disraeli seems to imagine. Ariosto, who raised such fine structures in his poetry, was asked, indeed, how he came to have no greater one when he built a house for himself; and he answered, that "palaces are easier built with words than stones." It was a pleasant answer, and fit for the interrogator: but Ariosto valued himself much upon the snug little abode which he did build, as may be seen by the inscription still remaining upon it at Ferrara;* and we will venture to say for

* See an engraving of the house itself, with its inscription, in the "Gallery of Portraits," No. 28, article "Ariosto." But it wants the garden-ground which belonged to it.

the cordial, tranquillity-loving poet, that he would rather live in such a house as that, and amuse himself with building palaces in his poetry, than have undergone the fatigue, and drawn upon himself the publicity, of erecting a princely mansion full of gold and marble. No mansion which he could have built would have equalled what he could fancy: and poets love nests from which they can take their flights, — not worlds of wood and stone to strut in, and give them a sensation. If so, they would have set their wits to get rich, and live accordingly; which none of them ever did yet, — at any rate, not the greatest. Ariosto notoriously neglected his "fortunes," in that sense of the word. Shakespeare had the felicity of building a house for himself, and settling in his native town; but, though the best *in* it, it was nothing equal to the "seats" outside of it (where the richer men of the district lived): and it appears to have been a "modest mansion;" not bigger, for instance, than a good-sized house in Red-Lion Street, or some other old quarter in the metropolis. Suppose he had set *his* great wits to rise in the state, and accumulate money, like Lionel Cranfield, for example, or Thomas Cromwell, the blacksmith's son. We know that any man who chooses to begin systematically with a penny, under circumstances at all favorable, may end with thousands. Suppose Shakespeare had done it: he might have built a house like a mountain. But he did not, it will be said, because he was a poet; and poets are not getters of money. Well, and for the same reason, poets do not care for the mightest things which money can get. It cannot get them health and freedom, and a life in the green fields, and mansions in Fairyland; and they prefer those, and a modest visible lodging.

Chaucer had a great large house to live in, — a castle, — because he was connected with royalty; but he does not delight to talk of such places: he is all for the garden, and the dasied fields, and a bower like a "pretty parlor." His mind was too big for a great house; which challenges measurement with its inmates, and is generally equal to them. He felt elbow-room, and heart-room, only out in God's air, or in the heart itself, or in the bowers built by Nature, and reminding him of the greatness of her love.

Spenser lived at one time in a castle, — in Ireland, — a piece of forfeited property, given him for political services; and he lived to repent it: for it was burnt in civil warfare, and his poor child burnt with it; and the poet was driven back to England, broken-hearted. But look at the houses he describes in his poems, — even he who was bred in a court, and loved pomp, after his fashion. He bestows the great ones upon princes and allegorical personages, who live in state and have many servants (for the largest houses, after all, are but collections of small ones, and of unfitting neighborhoods too); but his nests, his poetic bowers, his *deliciæ* and *amœnitates*, he keeps for his hermits and his favorite nymphs, and his flowers of courtesy: and observe how he delights to repeat the word "little," when describing them. His travellers come to "little valleys," in which, through the tree-tops, comes reeking up a "little smoke" (a "chearefull signe," quoth the poet), and —

> "To *little* cots in which the shepherds lie;"

and though all his little cots are not happy, yet he is ever happiest when describing them, should they be so, and showing in what sort of contentment his mind delighted finally to rest.

> "A *little* lowly heritage it was,
> Down in a dale, hard by a forest's side,
> Far from resort of people that did pass
> In travel to and fro. A *little* wide
> There was an holy chappell edifyde,
> Wherein the hermit dewly wont to say
> His holy things each morn and eventide:
> Thereby a crystall streame did gently play,
> Which from a sacred fountain wellèd forth alway.
>
> Arrivèd there, the *little* house they fill,
> Nor look for entertainment where none was;
> Rest is their feast, and all things at their will:
> *The noblest mind the best contentment has.*"

Milton, who built the Pandemonium, and filled it with—

> "A thousand demi-gods on golden seats,"

was content if he could but get a "garden-house" to live in, as it was called in his time; that is to say, a small house in the suburbs, with a bit of garden to it. He required nothing but a tree or two about him to give him "airs of Paradise." His biographer shows us that he made a point of having a residence of this kind. He lived as near as he could to the woodside and the fields, like his fellow-patriot, M. Beranger, who would have been the Andrew Marvell of those times, and adorned his great friend as the other did, or like his Mirth (l'Allegro) visiting his Melancholy.

And hear beloved Cowley, quiet and pleasant as the sound in his trees: "I never had any other desire so strong, and so like to covetousness, as that one which I have had always, — that I might be master at last of a *small* house and *large* garden, with very moderate conveniences joined to them, and there dedicate the remainder of my life only to the culture of them, and study of nature; and there, with no design beyond my wall, —

> 'Whole and entire to lie,
> In no unactive ease, and no unglorious poverty.'"
>
> *The Garden.*

"I confess," says he in another essay (on Greatness), "I love littleness almost in all things, — a little convenient estate, a little cheerful house, a little company, and a very little feast; and, if ever I were to fall in love again (which is a great passion, and therefore I hope I have done with it), it would be, I think, with prettiness, rather than with majestical beauty."

(What charming writing! — how charming *as* writing, as well as thinking! and charming in both respects, because it possesses the only real perfection of either, — truth of feeling.)

Cowley, to be sure, got such a house as he wanted, "at last," and was not so happy in it as he expected to be; but then it was because he did only get it "*at last*," when he was growing old, and was in bad health. Neither might he have ever been so happy in such a place as he supposed; (blessed are the poets, surely, in enjoying happiness even in imagination!) yet he would have been less comfortable in a house less to his taste.

Dryden lived in a house in Gerrard Street (then almost a suburb), looking, at the back, into the gardens of Leicester House, the mansion of the Sidneys. Pope had a nest at Twickenham, much smaller than the fine house since built upon the site; and Thomson, another at Richmond, consisting only of the ground-floor of the present house. Everybody knows what a rural house Cowper lived in. Shenstone's was but a farm adorned, and his bad health unfortunately hindered *him* from enjoying it. He married a house and grounds, poor man! instead of a wife; which was being very "one-sided" in his poetry; and he found them more expensive than Miss Dolman would have been. He had better have taken poor Maria first, and got a few domestic cares of a handsome sort, to keep him alive and moving. Most of the living poets are dwellers in cottages, except Mr. Rogers, who is rich, and has a mansion looking on one of the parks; but there it *does* look — upon grass and trees. He will have as much nature with his art as he can get. Next to a cottage of the most comfortable order, we should prefer, for our parts, if we must have servants and a household, one of those good old mansions of the Tudor age, or some such place, which looks like a sort of cottage-palace, and is full of old corners, old seats in the windows, and old memories. The servants, in such a case, would probably have grown old in one's family, and become friends; and this makes a great difference in the possible comfort of a great house. It gives it old family warmth.

A JOURNEY BY COACH.

A Fragment.

A FRIEND* and myself found ourselves, one showery August afternoon, sitting at the White Horse in Piccadilly, the sole occupants of the inside of an Oxford coach, and keeping such grave faces as sickness could help us to, in resistance of the almost unbearable tendency to laugh, produced by the crowd of fruit-sellers, pencil-men, pocket-book thrusters into your face, and other urgent philanthropists, who cannot conceive it possible how you can stir from London, unprovided from their especial stocks.

We confess we have a regard for these men, owing to their excessive energy, and the loudness with which they pursue the interests of their wives and families. We stand it out as long as we can; perhaps buy nothing, out of a secret admiration of what we seem to be disliking, and a sense of maintaining an honorable contest, — they with their tongues, and we with our faces, which we keep fixed on some object foreign to the matter in hand (the only way), and pretend to hold in a state of indifference, from which there is no hope. If we buy nothing, our conscience absolutely

* The late Mr. Egerton Webbe. Alas that we should so soon and unexpectedly be forced to say "late"!

twinges us; and yet how could we more honorably treat an honorable enemy? He clearly thinks it a matter of vigor and perseverance, — a regular battle: we take him at his word, and won't at all purchase. His object is to thrust his oranges into our pockets; ours, to keep our money there: his, to be loud, importunate, and successful; ours, to be still, insipid-looking, and of course successful also. We respect him so much, that we must needs maintain his respect for ourselves; and how are we to do this if we give in? He will think us weak fellows, — chaps that can't resist: so we do not care twopence for his wife and family, but intrench ourselves in a malignant benevolence towards our own. *Orangery* begins at home. But the only sure way is to fix your eyes on some other point, and say nothing. It is a battle won on your part by an intensity of indifference. You must not even look as if you disputed. You must fix your eyes on a shop-window; or on vacancy; or on the woman who is waiting for her husband; or the bundle which the other is hugging; or the dog who has just had a kick in the mouth, and is licking it with sedentary philosophy in a corner, looking at the same time about him; or you may watch the gentleman's face who has come half an hour too soon, but is afraid to go into a house to wait. If you look at your assailants, you only increase the vociferation; if you smile, they think you half won; if you object to the price, it is all over with you. Let your smile be internal, and your superiority immense, and not to be reached. Let them say to themselves, "That fellow must be a magistrate, or an inspector of police."

At length, a sudden bustle, and some creaking evidences on the part of the coach, announce that you are about to set off. Trunks lumber and "flop" overhead; all the outside passengers are seated; the box and its steps feel the weight of the ascending charioteer, as the axle-trees of their cars groaned under the gods of Homer; an unknown individual touches his hat, informing you that he has "seen to the things;" hasty anxieties are expressed for the box, the portmanteau, the carpet-bag; "all's right;" a kind domestic face is taken leave of with a moist eye (don't let any but the sick or the very masculine know it); and off we start, rattling with ponderous dance over the stones of Piccadilly.

We have never seen a description of the *inside* of a coach. It is generally too much occupied to be thought of, except as a collection of fellow-passengers. In the present instance, we had it all to ourselves, and could reconnoitre it: nobody, in summer-time, ever thinking, it seems, of going inside, except in cases of illness, and then very seldom; particularly if it is a wet night, and the "young woman" is to be sent down cheaply to Guinea Lodge. A mail-coach, in summer-time, may be defined, — a hollow box, with people outside of it. For upwards of two hundred miles, we had a series of coaches nearly all to our two selves, as if each of them had been a private carriage. We lounged in them, we changed corners, we put our legs up, and got acquainted with every part and particle of their accommodation. It is a tight kind of half-soft, half-hard thing, — is the inside of a coach; more hard than soft; not quite so convenient as it looks; "more

No than Yes," as the Italian said. The tight gray drugget looks compact and not uncomfortable, yet does not invite your headache to rest against it. The pockets seem as if they ought to contain more than they do: the pair of shoes won't go quite in. The floor has neither carpet nor straw, nor is it quite even; and the places to put things in under the seat are apt to baffle your attempts, if the things are at all large; and you do not want them for trifles. If you put your gloves or a few books on the seat, in a few minutes you find them gone off upon the floor. The drugget is occasionally varied with gay colors; and the windows are generally good, — pulling up and down with facility. In short, there is a show of liberality, in which you speedily discern a *skimping* saving, — the same spirit which spoils the building of modern houses as well as coaches. The old coaches, we may be certain, were larger and more generous, though they made less pretension, and went at a snail's pace in the comparison. We like "coaching" it, for our own parts; and should have been well content to live upon the road, in those patient antiques, instead of getting on at the present rate, and being impatient to arrive at some town, where we shall perhaps be equally restless. Not that we are insensible to the pleasure of driving fast. We like that too; it stirs the blood, and gives a sense of power: but every thing is a little too *smug* and hasty at present, and business-like, as though we were to be eternally getting on, and never realizing any thing but fidget and money, — the means instead of the end. We are truly in a state of transition, — of currency rather; and thank Heaven we are, and that it is transition only. Heaven forefend that the good planet should stop where it is, — at a Manchester millennium!

And we cannot take thoroughly to the modern, and, we hope, transitory coachman, compared with the humbler pretensions of his predecessor. We acknowledge his improvement in some respects. He wears gloves; has cleaner linen, and an opinion of himself; and is called "Sir" by the hostlers. He gathers the reins in his hands with a sort of half-gentility, — a certain retinence and composure of bearing; and gives answers in the style of a man who is not to be too much troubled, — a part-proprietor, or, for aught we know, corn-chandler, and cousin to Squire Jenks himself, who in less knowing times was called Farmer Jenks. He knows what belongs to the Diffusion of Coaches. You doubt, notwithstanding his red face, whether he could ever get in a passion, and swear; till, somebody bringing his authority into question, out comes the long-suppressed, natural, gin-drinking man of many weathers. Peace be to him, poor fellow! and a fit of illness that shall stop his drinking in time.

After all, however, our coach was a very good coach, and the coachmen as good also, — for aught that we recollect to the contrary. We are painting from the race in general. We had the inside, as we said before, all to ourselves: we had books, rapidity, fresh air, and one another's company. Good-natured Cowley was with us, in the shape of his delightful volume of Essays; Parnell, Shenstone, and others, not taxing the faculties overmuch, but good, chatting, inn-loving men; some Shakespeare, fit for all places, especially for one to which we were bound; a bit of Greek Anthology; some extracts from "Blackwood," "Fraser," "Tait," and the "New Monthly," chiefly consisting of delightful chat upon poets (of which more by and by); and a curious volume, little known, of miscellaneous prose by Armstrong, in which one of the best-natured men that ever lived appears to be one of the most caustic and querulous.

All these books and papers kept sliding every now and then from the seats, and set us laughing. The air was delightfully fresh and moist; the bits of black earth, spun up by the coach-wheels, danced merrily by the windows. We passed Hyde-Park Corner, famous for Pope's going to school; Knightsbridge, where Steele made Savage write the pamphlet that was to pay for their dinner; and are come in sight of Kensington, and Mrs. Inchbald's privacy, — a public-house.

But we must here give the reader breath; requesting his company with us next week.

A JOURNEY BY COACH.

CONTINUED.

"LIFE has few things better than this," said Dr. Johnson, on feeling himself settled in a coach, and rolling along the road.

"The pleasure is complete, sir," said Boswell; thinking to echo the sentiment of his illustrious friend, and leave no doubt about it.

"Why, no, sir," returned the doctor, who did not choose to be too much agreed with, *Boswellically*. "You have to arrive somewhere: there is to be an end of the pleasure. Sir, you have a melancholy anticipation."

We quote from memory, — probably with little justice to what was really said; but such was the gist of it. We confess we did not think with Johnson, in the present instance: for the friends we had left behind us, and the friends we were going to see, are both better things to live with than the fact of being on the road; and our health was not good enough to render the intermediate state of existence a perfect one. But where the circumstances are all favorable, or the change merely good for its own sake, we do thoroughly hold with the doctor, that few things in life are better than rolling along in a coach at your ease, looking out upon novelty, and feeling lord of your place and time.

And as to the melancholy of arriving somewhere, it has often struck us how unwise it is, in people not bound upon any journey's end more attractive than ordinary, to be in so much haste to reach there. People must exist *somewhere;* and where better (except with dear friends) than in the midst of scenes of nature, in fresh air, and in any easy state of movement? To be borne along, with no trouble, and yet without compulsion or mere passiveness, and with a sense of the power of commanding what you enjoy, is surely a pleasurable state of being both for body and mind. Let the reader nestle himself up in a corner of the coach, with his arms folded, and thorough room for his legs; and fancy it. Perhaps he shuts his eyes, and a balmy air comes breathing on the lids, while his body is carried jovially along, — jolted a little, occasionally, *without* jolting, — wafted over the fine English roads, now dashing at the hill, now going gentlier down it; spinning along a perfect level, or gently dipping into a bit of an undulation, and so up again, just enough to bend his chin a little closer, and remind him how smoothly the carriage is hung.

Verily an English stage-coach is a fine thing, and they do *not* "order these matters better in France." What we miss of our lively neighbors, when the coach has strangers in it, is their sociability; but when a couple of friends have the inside to themselves, as was the case in our instance, what more can be desired? No wonder the Spanish gentleman, when he saw such an equipage at his door, with its handsome horses instead of mules, its compact and comfortable self, its nice leather reins (not ropes, as they have in the South), its respectful and respectable coachman, and the royal arms to boot on the panels, thought he had been provided by government with the carriage of one of its nobles; and found it especially difficult to be convinced to the contrary, when he was seated in all its luxury, and smoothly scudding for London at the rate of ten miles an hour.

But to resume our setting out. Since writing our last, we had reason to believe that we had been misinformed respecting the site of Mrs. Inchbald's sequestered retirement, the public-house; and, on consulting her Memoirs by Mr. Boaden, we find that it was in the other Kensington Road, — the one from Oxford Street, — at No. 1, St. George's Terrace, near the chapel where Sterne lies. We have been told, that, somebody asking her how she came to lodge at a public-house, she said with great apparent simplicity, perhaps to mystify the inquirer, "They had very good beer there." We take this opportunity of observing, that, when we speak jestingly of this abode, we do it out of no disrespect to the memory of this excellent woman and admirable writer. She was an original in conduct as well as in writing, but all in a true and superior, not affected or mean spirit. She lived at a public-house because it was cheap, and had a good prospect; and she lived cheaply, because she gave her money away to poor friends and relations. She would pass a winter without a fire, the want of which she sometimes felt so as to make her "cry with cold," in order to be able to afford one to an ailing sister. O true Christian and noble creature! Thy love of superiority was full of heart! Angels, if angels could suffer, might so suffer for us, and be above us; and, what was wanting in our pity, we should supply with love.

Luckily, we do not lose sight of Mrs. Inchbald on this road. If her public-house was not where we supposed it, her last lodging-houses were at Kensington; and her last home, on this side heaven. But we shall come there presently.

We have passed Knightsbridge, once a terrible lonely place, of cut-throat reputation; and the "Cannon Brewery" (which an accomplished Spanish acquaintance of ours, on his coming into England, noted in his pocket-book, as presenting a curious specimen of English parlance, supposing that the casting of cannon was called *brewing* them); and the barracks, where tall dragoons are seen discoursing with little women; and have come into Kensington Gore, with Hyde Park again.

Hyde Park is associated with the reviews and the duels of latter generations; Kensington Gardens, with their court beauties and Sunday visitors; and the palace and suburb, with the court itself, or some connection of royalty, and with court wits and others. Gray came here to try to get rid of his last sickness; and here Arbuthnot lodged at one time, and Swift.

We have been thinking of courts and gay gardens, and had forgotten the church and its graves; and a shadow suddenly falls upon us in approaching it, reminding us of a melancholy portion of one of the most painful parts of our life. But a small angel sits smiling at us through it, with eyes earnest beyond its infancy; and we are rebuked by its better knowledge, and resume our patience, willingly admitting a new relief that has been lately afforded us by learning that Mrs. Inchbald lies in the same spot. It seems as if any kind of innocence both received and imparted a grace from its juxtaposition with such a woman. For her genius and fame are, of course, not what we are thinking of on the occasion: it is the fitness of the greater angel for sleeping by the side of the less. Mrs. Inchbald was very fond of Kensington. She resided there, or in the neighborhood, during the last ten or twelve years of her life: first at Turnham Green; then in St. George's Row (as above mentioned); then at No. 4, Earl's Place, opposite Holland House: then in Leonard's Place; then in Sloane Street (at No. 148); and, lastly, in Kensington House, a Catholic boarding-establishment, where she died. She was fond of Kensington for its healthiness, its retirement, its trees and prospects, its Catholic accommodations (for she was a liberal believer of that church); but not least, we suspect, for a reason which Mr. Boaden's interesting biography has not mentioned; namely, the interment, in Kensington churchyard, of the eminent physician, Dr. Warren, for whom, in her thirty-eighth year, and in the twelfth year of a widowhood graced by genius, beauty, and refusals of other marriages, she entertained a secret affection, so young and genuine, that she would walk up and down Sackville Street, where he lived, purely to get a glimpse of the light in his window. Her heart was so excellent, and accustomed to live on aspirations so noble, that we have not the least doubt this was one of her great ties to Kensington, and that she looked forward with something of an angelical delight to the hour when she should repose in the earth near the friend whose abode she could not partake while living.

We beg the reader to pardon a digression longer than we shall usually indulge in, for the sake of the feelings of gratitude and admiration just re-excited in us by a perusal of the life of this extraordinary woman, the authoress of some of the most amusing comedy and pathetic narrative in the language; a reformer, abhorring violence; a candid confesser of her own faults, not in a pick-thank and deprecating style, but honest and heartfelt (for they hurt her craving for sympathy); an admirable kinswoman and friend nevertheless, — most admirable, as we have just seen; the creator of the characters of "Dorriforth" and "Miss Milman;" and the writer of a book ("Nature and Art") which a woman, worthy to have been her friend, put during his childhood into the hands of the writer of these pages; to the no small influence, he believes, of opinions which he afterwards aspired to advocate, however imperfectly he may have proved his right to do so.

Dr. Warren, a man as good as he was intelligent, is in the recollection of many. We have heard, from a lady who remembers him, that he was a very gentlemanly man, with all the wise suavity of the genuine physician, — not of a healthy complexion, but with very fine eyes. And we learn from another, that his searching and refined look, his professional skill, his power to attach affection, and, alas! his delicacy of health, are hereditary in the name.

Truly, love keeps one a long while lingering at the door; and we shall never get on with our journey at this rate.

We must begin again next week, and *move faster!*

A JOURNEY BY COACH.

CONTINUED.

Holland House and its Memories. — Formal new Buildings in the Roads near London. — New Public-houses inferior to the Old ones. — Hammersmith and its Legend, &c. — Turnham Green. — Passages from Gay and the "Mayor of Garrat." — Brentford. — Cavaliers and Puritans. — Sion House. — Osterley Park. — A Halt at an Inn-door.

THE traveller, in passing Holland House, must try to get as long a glimpse of it as he can; and if he has any fancy, and is a reader, the old house will glow to him like a painted window. Visions of wits and beauties will flash upon his eyes, from the times of Elizabeth and James the First down to this present November, 1835; with more, we trust, to come. Perhaps there has not been a set of men, eminent in their day, who, for the most part, have not visited at that house. It was built by the Cope Family in 1607; then possessed by the Earl of Holland, one of the favorites of Charles the First's wife, Henrietta Maria; then by the Commonwealth, whose general, Fairfax, made it his head-quarters on one occasion; then by the Holland Family again, through whom, by his marriage with the Countess of Warwick and Holland, it became the residence of Addison, who died there; then by a descendant of the family, who sold it to Henry Fox, afterwards Lord Holland; and it has since remained in the possession of his successors.

Here Charles Fox spent his childhood with a good-natured father, who helped him to remain something of a child all his life, — the luckiest thing that can happen to a great man. Here, in all probability, visited the Sucklings and Lady Carlisles, of the time of Charles the First; here the Buckinghams of the two Charleses, with all the wits of those days; here, certainly, Steele and his fellow-associates of Addison; here Walpole and Hanbury Williams, and the beauties of the Richmond and other families; here the Jeffreys, Burkes, and Sheridans; and here the Broughams, Byrons, Rogerses, Campbells, Thomas Moores, and all the other Whig genius of the present age, attracted by the congenial abilities and the flowing hospitality of the biographer of Lope de Vega, — a true nephew of Charles Fox, — a nobleman gracing, and helping to secure, his order, because he sympathizes with all ranks. We never pass Holland House (and we pass it often, and often look up at it from its gate) without wishing a blessing and long life to the man whose possession of so fair a place it is not in the nature of the poorest honest man to grudge him.*

And the house is worth looking at, too, for its own sake. It is a curious specimen of the style of architecture in the reign of Elizabeth and James; and, to our feelings, not less comfortable-looking than curious; for it gives one the idea of a multitude of snug, straggling rooms, situated in all sorts of corners and

* While revising this sheet for the press, we have to lament the death of this most genial and excellent man, the delight of all who knew him, and the friend of the world.

staircases: and there is a noble library, be sure; besides plenty of family and other pictures.

Adieu to snug, old, picturesque Holland House, with its hundred visions from the windows; for we must push on. The worst of the roads near London is, that, for a long while, you seem to be neither in London nor in the country. You think you have got into the latter, when some long formal row of houses, some "Prospect Place" or "Paradise Row," or, worse than that, some spick and span new, yellowbrick set, convinces you to the contrary; and the Paradise Row, perhaps, has no gardens, and the Prospect Place no prospect. Paradise Row was doubtless Paradise *once;* but the Adam and Eve have been driven out by the taste of bricklaying; and Prospect Place had a "view," till "Smith's Terrace," or some such interloper, came sidling in front of it with forty new tenements, and impudently deprived it of the beatific vision of its cow-field.

What we particularly hate in the new buildings about London is the rebuilt or furbished-up public-houses. They think themselves very fine, with their new, flat faces, and their golden letters on blue grounds; and the people have doubtless got a lift in the world, and are mighty "respectable-like" and serious and disagreeable; or else they are at their wit's end to pay for the finery, and drink and swear worse than Tom Dykes over the way, whose wife died a month after she had had a battle with him. Perhaps, to mend the matter, they cut down the tree in front. The place then becomes all as flat as need be, and worth nobody's looking at, except a bricklayer's.

Nobody wishes to stop at it, except the mere drinker, or the mere man of business: and he is for getting on as fast as possible, as he well may; for what is the use of his stopping anywhere? For our parts, give us the good, old, snug, picturesque public-house, which had, and in remoter places still has, the great tree before it, with a bench, and the old swinging sign, that sings or creaks in the winds on winter-nights; and the landlord, not above nor below his respectable calling,—hearty as the punch-bowl in his window, and clean as his sanded floor. We have touched upon the interior of such a house in the first article of our journey; and we never pass its outside without thinking what a picture it makes, and how well it would look *in* a picture. But what has the "Jolly Gardener," or the "Shepherd and Shepherdess," or the "Bull," or "Robin Hood," or the "Hand and Flower," or the "Angel," or the "Maiden's Head," to do with a great, flat-faced, commercial, dusty road, and rows of new houses? May a devil's blessing (as the philanthropist said) light on those who do not endeavor (like proper reformers, as *we* are) to bring the new beautifully out of the old, and thus to retain what is good, while they are making things better!

But we are anticipating; for we are not to halt yet: we have not got far enough. We pass the lane turning to Acton, on the right hand, and to Fulham on the left; and are in Hammersmith, famous for its ghost, and its suspension-bridge, and the abode of Richardson. Here is also a convent of nuns; a rare sight in England, especially so near the metropolis. They are of the order of Benedictines; nay, we believe, of the branch of Visitandines,—the same that were so scandalized at the worldly knowledge of their famous parrot, *Vert-Vert*, yet could not find it in their good hearts to detest him. (See *Œuvres de Gresset*, or the translations in various collections of poetry; or in "Fraser's Magazine" a few months back.) We have met with a legend somewhere, respecting the origin of the name of Hammersmith, which relates that two gigantic sisters residing there built the churches at Putney and Fulham; and that they threw over to one another, as they wanted it, across the river, a stupendous *hammer*. It is a pity when a name of obvious solution puts an end even to the most improbable fiction. Hammersmith was evidently the abode of some country blacksmith in old time, and probably consisted of this solitary shop, the first that was met with on the high-road going from London.

The person, whoever he was, that played the part of a ghost in this village some years back, and was the occasion of an innocent man's being shot, has probably repented of his foolish prank. The length and bitterness of his regret, by this time, will have earned him a right to forgive himself.

We have mentioned that Mrs. Inchbald once resided at Turnham Green, the next place from Hammersmith. It is famous for the blunder attributed to Goldsmith about the bad peas. He had heard the joke about taking them from Hammersmith "to *turn 'em green;*" and is said, in repeating it, to have substituted the words "*make 'em green*" *for* "*turn 'em.*" On coming from Kensington, you catch views of

Harrow on the Hill, where Garth lies; and, betwixt Hammersmith and Brentford, you look on the right towards Acton, where Lady Wortley Montagu lived; and Ealing, where her cousin Fielding once resided. Gay has mentioned this road, in his epistle to the Earl of Burlington, entitled a "Journey to Exeter:"—

> "While you, my lord, bid stately piles ascend,

(Burlington House, in Piccadilly, which we have passed, was one of his building,)

> Or in your Chiswick bowers enjoy your friend,

(Chiswick lies a mile out of the road to the left, as you enter Turnham Green,)

> Where Pope unloads the boughs within his reach.
> The purple vine, blue plum, and blushing peach,
> I journey far. You knew fat bards might tire,
> And, mounted, sent me forth, your trusty squire.
> 'Twas on the day when city dames repair
> To take their weekly dose of Hyde-Park air,
> When forth we trot: no carts the road infest;
> For still, on Sundays, country horses rest.

(Except when they are used for chaises and other vehicles.)

> Thy gardens, Kensington, we leave unseen;
> Through Hammersmith jog on to Turnham Green,—
> That Turnham Green which dainty pigeons fed,
> But feeds no more; for Solomon is dead:

(Solomon was a breeder of pigeons:)

> Three dusty miles reach Brentford's tedious town,
> For dirty streets and white-legged chickens known."

But Foote has blown the finest mock-heroical trumpet in celebration of this district, in his famous banter upon the city-militia. The passage is very ludicrous; so the reader shall have it as he goes in his coach: for, besides those who at present accompany ourselves, we hope these papers may be taken with them by some other readers, by and by, who happen to go the same road.

Sir Jacob. Well, major, our wars are done: the rattling drum and squeaking fife now wound our ears no more.

Major Sturgeon. True, Sir Jacob; our corps is disembodied: so the French may sleep in security.

Sir J. But, major, was it not rather late in life for you to enter upon the profession of arms?

Major S. A little awkward in the beginning, Sir Jacob: the great difficulty they had was to get me to turn out my toes; but use — use reconciles all them kind of things. Why, after my first campaign, I no more minded the noise of the guns than a flea-bite.

Sir J. No!

Major S. No. There is more made of these matters than they merit. For the general good, indeed, I am glad of the peace; but as to my single self — and yet we have had some desperate duty, Sir Jacob.

Sir J. No doubt.

Major S. Oh! such marchings and counter-marchings, from Brentford to Ealing, from Ealing to Acton, from Acton to Uxbridge; the dust flying, sun scorching, men sweating! Why, there was our last expedition to Hounslow: that day's work carried off Major Molasses. Bunhill Fields never saw a braver commander. He was an irreparable loss to the service.

Sir J. How came that about?

Major S. Why, it was partly the major's own fault. I advised him to pull off his spurs before he went upon action; but he was resolute, and would not be ruled.

Sir J. Spirit; zeal for the service.

Major S. Doubtless. But to proceed: in order to get our men in good spirits, we were quartered at Thistleworth the evening before. At daybreak, our regiment formed at Hounslow town's end, as it might be about here. The major made a fine disposition: on we marched, the men all in high spirits, to attack the gibbet where Gardel is hanging; but turning down a narrow lane to the left, as it might be about there, in order to possess a pig-sty, that we might take the gallows in flank, and, at all events, secure a retreat, who should come by but a drove of fat oxen from Smithfield! The drums beat in the front, the dogs barked in the rear, the oxen set up a gallop: on they came thundering upon us, broke through our ranks in an instant, and threw the whole corps into confusion.

Sir J. Terrible!

Major S. The major's horse took to his heels: away he scoured o'er the heath. That gallant commander stuck both his spurs into his flank, and, for some time, held by his mane; but, in crossing a ditch, the horse threw up his head, gave the major a douse in the chops, and plumped him into a gravel-pit, just by the powder-mills.

Sir J. Dreadful!

Major S. Whether from the fall or the fright, the major moved off in a month. Indeed, it was an unfortunate day for us all.

Sir J. As how?

Major S. Why, as Capt. Cucumber, Lieut. Pattypan, Ensign Tripe, and myself, were returning to town in the Turnham-Green stage, we were stopped near the Hammersmith Turnpike, and robbed and stripped by a single footpad.

This is very laughable; but, whatever may be the airs occasionally given themselves by civic heroes, their actual service in the field has proved itself to be no joke; as poor Charles the First found to his cost, and in this very spot. In an encounter with the London forces, Prince Rupert left eight hundred cavaliers dead upon Turnham Green; and, in the subsequent engagement at Brentford, the same gentleman, according to a pamphlet issued by the Puritans, said, "God damn them! the Devil was in their powder."* We are the more willing to vindicate the dignity of these our warlike suburbs, because, to "own the soft impeachment," we "ourself," when time was, have been a gallant volunteer, doing dreadful "field-day" in the same neighborhood, and tearing loaves out of bakers' baskets, and spigots out of the barrels in beer-cellars, in the very rage of hunger and thirst and lawless campaigning.

Between Brentford and Ealing, Lysons informs us that elephants' bones and similar phenomena have

* "A true relation of the battail at Brentford, the 12th of November, between his Majesty's army and the Parliament army; and how the cavaliers swore God damn them, the Devil was in their powder." Title of a pamphlet in the British Museum, mentioned by Lysons in his "Environs of London." We have forgotten to refer to the page and volume.

been dug up, — evidences of a former state of climate in this quarter of the world, when our planet was toasting a different cheek at the sun.

The celebrated engagement between the King's and Parliament's forces took place at the south-west of Brentford, near Sion House. A Sunday intervened; and it is said that the quantity of "victuals" sent out from London to feed the worthy city belligerents was immense.

This town takes its name from the little river Brent, which helps to give such a pretty look to the entrance of the village of Hendon. Fuller speaks of a gardener living here at the beginning of the seventeenth century, who, at seventy-six years of age, could afford, in the course of three days, to lose more than sixty ounces of blood, to cure him of an inflammation of the lungs; which it did, — "a most eminent instance," adds he, "against those who endeavor to prove the decay of the world, because men cannot spare so much by blood-letting as in former ages."

Sion House was originally a Bridgetine convent, in which monks and nuns lived under the same roof, though in separate cloisters. At the dissolution of the monasteries by Henry the Eighth, it was very ill spoken of; not the less, perhaps, for being accused of siding with his antagonist, the Maid of Kent. Katharine Howard was confined in this house before her execution. Queen Mary made Sir Henry Sidney (Sir Philip's father) keeper of the parks and woods; and after being again monasticized, and again dissolved, Elizabeth gave the estate to the Northumberland Family, with whom it has since remained. The

Saccharissa of Waller (Dorothy Sidney, a granddaughter of Henry, Earl of Northumberland) was born there.

Osterley House, the seat of the Jerseys, a little further on, upon the other side of the way, was built by the celebrated merchant, Sir Thomas Gresham. It was subsequently occupied by Sir Edward Coke, by the Desmond Family, and by Sir William Waller, the Parliamentary general; and, at the beginning of the last century, became the property of Sir Francis Child, the banker, whose descendants brought it, by marriage, into the Jersey Family. Two curious stories are told of it; one by Fuller in his "Worthies," the other in the Strafford Letters. The latter we copy from Lysons, who relates them both; but we prefer hearing good, old, quaint, eloquent Fuller speak for himself.

"Osterley House," says he, "now Sir William Waller's, must not be forgotten, built in a park by Sir Thomas Gresham, who here magnificently entertained and lodged Queen Elizabeth. Her majesty found fault with the court of this house as too great; affirming, 'that it would appear more handsome, if divided with a wall in the middle.'

"What doth Sir Thomas, but in the night-time sends for workmen to London (money commands all things), who so speedily and silently apply their business, that the next morning discovered that court double, which the night had left single before. It is questionable whether the queen next day was more contented with the conformity to her fancy, or more pleased with the surprise and sudden performance thereof; whilst her courtiers disported themselves with their several expressions, some avowing it was no wonder he could so soon *change a building* who could *build a 'Change;* others (reflecting on some known differences in this knight's family) affirmed 'that any house is easier *divided* than *united.*'"*

The other story is thus quoted by Lysons from the letters above mentioned: "Young Desmond (says Mr. Garrard, writing to Lord Wentworth), who married one of the co-heirs of Sir Michael Stanhope, came one morning to York House, where his wife had long lived with the duchess during his two years' absence beyond the seas, and hurried her away, half undressed, much against her will, into a coach, and so carried her away into Leicestershire. At Brickhill he lodged, where she, in the night, put herself into milkmaid's clothes, and had likely to make her escape, but was discovered. Madam Christian, whom your lordship knows, said that my Lord of Desmond was the first that ever she heard of that ran away with his own wife."

The case has often happened, where money was concerned. The countess afterwards came to Osterley Park with her husband, and bore him a numerous family.

It should have been mentioned, in justice to Brentford, that we did not observe the "dirty street" in it mentioned by Gay: at least, the High Street looked smart and comfortable. All the thoroughfares in towns near London, and indeed almost all that we saw of any consequence in our journey, have wonderfully

* "Worthies of England," vol. ii. 1811, p. 45.

plucked up, and *smugged* themselves, of late years. The communication which is now grown so general between all parts of the country, renders all of them, in some measure, like neighbors; and what is done by one town, for the sake of neatness and ascendency, gets done by another. You see a regular pavement, smart London-looking shops, a circulating library, milliner's, watchmaker's, &c.; and the coach halts at a fine-looking inn, with large coach-yard, door, and other appurtenances, of the newest town fashion; out of which comes a smart waiter or landlord, no more anxious or civil in his countenance than the waiter of a well-to-do inn ought to be, and who does not seem to care whether you lunch or not. Meanwhile "miss," if she is pretty or well-dressed, gives a look out at the threshold, with an eye still more indifferent, and glancing everywhere but at the faces she is thinking of. Passengers descend to stretch their legs for ten minutes, the inside and out reconnoitring one another; the "young woman" remains by her bundle; the gentleman in the travelling-cap longs to know where the gentleman in the shooting-jacket is going, but, not having dined yet, has not acquired confidence enough to speak; and the invalid gentleman eats a biscuit, or extremely declines it.

A JOURNEY BY COACH.

CONCLUDED.

Coach-horses.—What do they think of the Coach?—Hounslow; its Thieves and Gunpowder.—Desideratum in Fighting.—The Wheat of Heston.—Singular Fertility of Berkshire and Buckinghamshire in illustrious Memories.—Extinction of the Highwayman.

HEN a coach sets off again from its stoppage at an inn-door, there is a sense of freshness and recommencement: the inside passengers settle themselves in their corners, or interchange legs, or take a turn on the outside; the outside adjust themselves to their seats and their bits of footing; the young woman looks, for the ninety-ninth time, to her box; the coachman is indifferent and scientific; he has the ease of power in his face; he shakes the reins; throws out a curve or so of knowing whip, as an angler does his line; and the horses begin to ply their never-ending jog. A horse's hind-leg on the road, to any eye looking down upon it, seems as if it would jaunt on for ever; the muscle works in the thigh; the mane at the same time dances a little bit; the hock-joint looks intensely angular, and not to be hit (it is horrible to think of wounding it); the hoof bites into the earth; wheels and legs seem made to work together like machinery; and on go the two patient creatures, they know not why nor whither, chewing the unsatisfactory bit, wondering (if they wonder at all) why they may not hold their heads down, and have tails longer than five inches; and occasionally giving one another's noses a consolatory caress. It is curious to see sometimes how this affection seems to be all on one side. One of the horses goes dumbly talking, as it were, to the other, and giving proofs of the pleasure and comfort it takes in its society; while the other, making no sort of acknowledgment, keeps the "even tenor of its way," turning neither to the right nor left, nor condescending to give or receive the least evidences of the possibility of a satisfaction. It seems to say, "You may be as amiable and patient as you please: for my part, I am resolved to be a mere piece of the machinery, and to give these fellows behind us no reason whatsoever to suppose that I make any sentimental compromise with their usurpations over us."

Horses in a coach must certainly be the most patient or the most indifferent or the most unthinking of animals. The mule seems to have an opinion of his own: he is not to be driven so easily. The dog (till the new act) passed a horrible, unsatisfied time of it under the butcher's or baker's go-cart. Harnessed elephants would be inconvenient. They would be for re-adjusting their buckles, and making inquiries with their trunks into the behavior of the postilion. They might, to be sure, help with the other trunks, and perform the part of half-horse, half-hostler. The llama of Peru has inconvenient tricks, if you ill use him; and so has the camel. But the horse, when once he is ground well into the road, seems to give up having any sort of mind of his own; that is to say, if he ever had any, except what his animal spirits made to be mistaken for it: for the breeding of horses is such in England, that, generally speaking, when they are not all blood and fire, they seem nothing but stupid acquiescence, without will, without curiosity, without the power of being roused into resistance, except, poor souls! when their last hour is come, and non-resistance itself can go no further, but lies down to die. We dock their tails, to subject them to the very flies; fasten their heads back, to hinder them from seeing their path; and put blinkers at their eyes, for fear of their getting used to the phenomena of the carriage and wheels behind them. What must they think (if they think at all) of the eternal mystery thus tied to their bodies, and rattling and lumbering at their heels? of the load thus fastened to them day by day, going the same road for no earthly object (intelligible to the horse capacity), and every now and then depositing, and taking up, other animals who walk on their hind-legs, and occasionally come and stroke their noses, kick their bellies, and gift them with iron shoes?

Well, circumstances drive us, as we drive the horses,—perhaps with as many smiling remarks on the part of other beings, at our thinking as little of the matter: so we must be moving on.

Hounslow (the stage we have now come to) is a good place for setting us upon reflections on horse and man, not merely by reason of the number of accommodations for both those travellers, but because of its celebrity at various times for its horse-races, its highwaymen, and its powder-mills. The series of heaths here from Hounslow to Bagshot are the scenes of the favorite robberies and stage-coach alarms of the last century. The novels and Newgate calendars are full of them. Nor is the district without its historical minacities. Here poor James the Second got up a camp to resist his subjects with; and must needs take his queen and his daughter Anne to dine there, to let them see how victorious he was going to be: nay, he wrote to the Prince of Orange upon the fineness of his troops; which the latter accordingly came over to congratulate him upon, as William the Third.

"Am I to have the honor of taking the air with you, sir, this evening upon the heath?" says one of the heroes of the "Beggar's Opera," to their noble Capt. *Mac*-HEATH; who derived his title, observe, from that ground of his exploits. "I drink a dram now and then with the stage-coachmen, in the way of friendship and intelligence; and I know, that, about this time, there will be passengers upon the western road who are worth speaking with."

And then follows a generous conversation about honor and fidelity, with certain glimpses of the interior of their cabinet policy; and the meeting concludes, instead of a ministerial dinner, with that glorious song, "Let us take the road," the music of which is justly "borrowed for the occasion," like a crown-jewel, from Handel's "March in Scipio." We dare confidently appeal to any ingenuous reader, who has heard it sung, and who has seen those "great irregular spirits," in their exaltation and ragged coats, passing by their leader with step and chorus, and taking their hats off, one by one, to his own elegantly lifted beaver, whether there is much difference, if any, between those mutual acknowledgments of energy and a great purpose, and others which take place on more public occasions. For our parts, we confess, as Sir Philip Sidney did of the ballad of "Chevy Chace," that we never hear it but we feel our "heart moved as with the sound of a trumpet;" and it raised a late noble lord twenty-fold in our opinion, nay, let us see that he had a truly "statesman-like" view of things, and an heroical cast in his character, when we heard that he was a great admirer of this song and of the whole opera. We have been told that he not only applauded it in public, but would get ladies to play it to him on the piano-forte, and hum over the airs himself with an exquisite superiority to his incompetency.*

Hounslow Heath is not a place which the old gentleman in the play would like to live in, who made such a fearful construction of a metaphor in a letter,

* Lord Castlereagh. We forget who told us the anecdote, and are not in the way of ascertaining the truth of it; but we have heard other stories of his good-nature, that render it likely. His lordship, like so many other statesmen of all parties, was the victim of a perplexed state of society, which seems of necessity to divide a man into two contradictory beings, — the public and the private; and, unfortunately, he did not see that this state was a transitory one, and not the inevitable condition of humanity. It is not likely, indeed, that he would refine upon this speculation in ordinary, or perhaps think of it at all. He was too busy, and, as it appeared to him, too successful. But there is no knowing how much thought and wonder crowded into his brain before he died, and found him unprepared to entertain them. Peace to his memory and his mistakes, and to those of all of us! In spite of his errors, he had something noble in his nature as well as in his countenance. We shall never thoroughly know how to master the circumstances that make us what we are, till we learn to leave off fighting with and reproaching one another.

and was always fancying that he and his were "all to be blown up." A very serious blowing up does in fact occasionally take place here, strewing the limbs and heads of the manufactures of gunpowder about the place, as if in rebuke of their trade. It is a pity that science does not hasten that most blessed of all its discoveries, which was talked of the other day, and which is to settle any two contending armies in ten minutes by blowing them respectively to atoms! They have only to meet, it seems, and give the word, and at the first explosion they are abolished; that is to say, provided one of them does not contrive to speak first: so that war would be reduced to a race for the first word, and the most precipitate speaker be the conqueror crowned with laurel. In a little while, it is clear that there would be no war at all; and then mankind, out of pure unheroical necessity, would be forced to be reasonable in their disputes, and let common sense be the arbiter. At present, the grand thing is to say, "*You* lie," and "*You* lie," and then to fall pell-mell together by the ears, and be the death of thousands of your fellow-creatures, to the sound of drum and trumpet. There is something fine in this, undoubtedly, especially for those who have to pay for it, or who are burnt, maimed, slaughtered, or sent to the hospital, in the process. But somehow it puts the very conquerors upon grave faces, and makes them feel like slaves to an evil thing, and keeps up the belief in the "vale of tears;" and people in their senses and cool moments prefer the idea of a healthy condition of humanity, and a game at cricket on a green. But railroads will be the peace-makers.

Hounslow Heath is to the left of our road: let us give a glance to the right, and refresh ourselves with thinking of that peaceful agriculturul district stretching from this parish to Harrow-on-the-Hill, and famous for the finest wheat in England. Queen Elizabeth had her bread from it. Fuller has recorded one end of it in his prose, and Drayton the other in his poetry.

"The best (wheat) in England," says Fuller, "groweth in the vale lying south of Harrow-on-the-Hill, nigh Hesson (Heston, the parish in which Hounslow lies), where Providence for the present hath fixed my habitation; so that the king's bread was formerly made of the fine flower thereof. Hence it was that Queen Elizabeth received no composition from the villages thereabouts, but took her wheate in kinde for her own pastry and bakehouse." *

"As Coln came on along, and chanced to cast her eye
Upon that neighboring hill where Harrow stands so high,
She Peryvale perceived, pranked up with wreaths of wheat,
And with exulting terms thus glorying in her seat:
'Why should not I be coy, and of my beauties nice,
Since this my goodly grain is held of highest price?
No manchet can so well the courtly palate please
As that made of the meal fetched from my fertile leas,'" &c.
DRAYTON'S *Polyolbion,* Song xiv.

Hounslow, whatever be its reputation, is in a truly glorious neighborhood. Draw a circle of a few miles round Windsor, and you have Cowley at Chertsey, Pope at Twickenham and at Windsor Forest, the Earl of Surrey in the Castle, Gray at Stoke Pogeis and

* "Worthies of England," vol. ii. p. 34.

at Eton, Milton at Horton, and *Magna Charta* at Runnymede. Buckinghamshire and Berkshire (with the exception of London) comprise perhaps the most illustrious district in England, unless Shakespeare alone raises Warwickshire above them; and the road in this quarter leads even to him, besides visiting Chaucer by the way. But Chaucer is also to be found in Berkshire, at Donnington Castle; Spenser in Buckinghamshire, at Whaddon, with his friend Lord Grey, to whom he was secretary; Shakespeare himself (as far as one of his most living creations is concerned) at Windsor, with Falstaff and the Merry Wives; Milton at Horton aforesaid, where he passed much of his youth: and, besides others before mentioned, we have Hampden at Hampden; Burke and Waller at Beaconsfield; Hooker at Drayton-Beauchamp; Cowper at Olney; Denham at Cooper's Hill; Hales, Wotton, and half the education of England, at Eton, — the whole weight of Windsor Castle and its memories; and at Wantage we have Alfred the Great, a world of a man in himself. Doubtless there are more honors for the two counties; but we happen to be writing without the first volume of Fuller, and these are all we can recollect. They include three out of the four great poets of England, as regards residence of some duration, — a thing that can be said of no other district of equal length, the metropolis excepted; and it is curious, that, within a segment of it, the very names of the towns and villages seem resolved to be literary and renowned, comprising Denham, Drayton, Cowley, Milton, Hampden, and Penn. We are mistaken if we have not seen a stage-coach enter London with three of these names upon its panel, — we think, Denham, Drayton, and Cowley.

We have omitted to observe how completely the Macheath order of highwaymen has gone out, — he who used to be mounted on horseback, and stop coaches, and put half a dozen people in fear of their lives. Guards, rapidity of driving, and other facilities of self-defence, the publicity of the roads, quickness of communication, &c., have extinguished him. He is as completely abolished as the wolves. No more can he swagger and bully, and call himself Captain, and seduce innkeepers' daughters, and be hung like a man of spirit. He is a sneaker now round the gaming-tables, or rides on the coach which he used to stop, and filches bankers' conveyances.

[These articles were cut short by the stoppage of the journal in which they appeared.]

INEXHAUSTIBILITY OF THE SUBJECT OF CHRISTMAS.

O many things have been said of late years about Christmas, that it is supposed by some there is no saying more. O they of little faith! What! do they suppose that every thing has been said that *can* be said about any one Christmas thing?

About beef, for instance?

About plum-pudding?

About mince-pie?

About holly?

About ivy?

About rosemary?

About mistletoe? (Good God! what an immense number of things remain to be said about mistletoe!)

About Christmas Eve?

About hunt-the-slipper?

About hot cockles?

About blind-man's-buff?

About shoeing the wild-mare?

About thread-the-needle?

About he-can-do-little-that-can't-do-this?

About puss-in-the-corner?

About snap-dragon?
About forfeits?
About Miss Smith?
About the bell-man?
About the waits?
About chilblains?
About carols?
About the fire?
About the block on it?
About school-boys?
About their mothers?
About Christmas-boxes?
About turkeys?
About Hogmany?
About goose-pie?
About mumming?
About saluting the apple-trees?
About brawn?
About plum-porridge?
About hobby-horse?
About hoppings?
About wakes?
About "feed-the-dove"?
About hackins?
About yule-doughs?
About going-a-gooding?
About loaf-stealing?
About *julklaps?* (Who has exhausted that subject, we should like to know?)
About wad-shooting?
About elder-wine?
About pantomimes?

About cards?
About New-Year's Day?
About gifts?
About wassail?
About Twelfth-cake?
About king and queen?
About characters?
About eating too much?
About aldermen?
About the doctor?
About all being in the wrong?
About charity?
About all being in the right?
About faith, hope, and endeavor?
About the greatest plum-pudding for the greatest number?

Esto perpetua, — that is, faith, hope, and charity, and endeavor; and plum-pudding enough by and by, all the year round, for everybody that likes it. Why that should not be the case, we cannot see, — seeing that the earth is big, and human kind teachable, and God very good, and inciting us to do it. Meantime, gravity apart, we ask anybody whether any of the above subjects are exhausted; and we inform everybody, that all the above customs still exist in some parts of our beloved country, however unintelligible they may have become in others. But to give a specimen of the non-exhaustion of any one of their topics.

Beef, for example. Now, we should like to know who has exhausted the subject of the fine old roast Christmas piece of beef, from its original appearance in the meadows as part of the noble sultan of the herd, glorious old Taurus, — the lord of the sturdy brow and ponderous agility, a sort of thunderbolt of a beast, well chosen by Jove to disguise in, one of Nature's most striking compounds of apparent heaviness and unencumbered activity, — up to its contribution to the noble Christmas-dinner, smoking from the spit, and flanked by the outposts of Bacchus. John Bull (cannibalism apart) hails it like a sort of relation. He makes it part of his flesh and blood; glories in it; was named after it; has it served up, on solemn occasions, with music and a hymn, as it was the other day at the royal city dinner: —

> "Oh the roast beef of old England!
> And oh the old English roast beef!"

"*And* oh!" observe; not merely "oh!" again; but "and" with it; as if, though the same piece of beef, it were also another, — another and the same, — cut, and come again; making two of one, in order to express intensity and reduplication of satisfaction: —

> "Oh the roast beef of old England!
> *And* oh the old English roast beef!"

We beg to assure the reader, that a whole *Seer* might be written on this single point of the Christmas-dinner; and "shall we be told" (as orators exclaim), "and this, too, in a British land," that the subject is "*exhausted*"!

Then plum-pudding! What a word is that! how plump, and plump again! How round and repeated and plenipotential! (There are two *p*'s, observe, in plenipotential; and so there are in plum-pudding. We love an exquisite fitness, — a might and wealth of adaptation.) Why, the whole round cheek of universal childhood is in the idea of plum-pudding; ay, and the weight of manhood, and the plenitude of the majesty of city dames. Wealth itself is symbolized by the least of its fruity particles. "A plum" is a city fortune, — a million of money. He (the old boy, who has earned it) —

"Puts in his thumb,

videlicet, into his pocket,

And pulls out a plum,
And says, What a *good man* am I!"

Observe a little boy at a Christmas-dinner, and his grandfather opposite him. What a world of secret similarity there is between them! How hope in one, and retrospection in the other, and appetite in both, meet over the same ground of pudding, and understand it to a nicety! How the senior banters the little boy on his third slice! and how the little boy thinks within himself that he dines that day as well as the senior! How both look hot and red and smiling, and juvenile. How the little boy is conscious of the Christmas-box in his pocket! (of which, indeed, the grandfather jocosely puts him in mind;) and how the grandfather is quite as conscious of the plum, or part of a plum, or whatever fraction it may be, in his own! How he incites the little boy to love money and good dinners all his life! and how determined the little boy is to abide by his advice, — with a secret addition in favor of holidays and marbles, — to which there is an analogy, in the senior's mind, on the side of trips to Hastings, and a game at whist! Finally, the old gentleman sees his own face in the pretty smooth one of the child; and if the child is not best pleased at his proclamation of the likeness (in truth, is horrified at it, and thinks it a sort of madness), yet nice observers, who have lived long enough to see the wonderful changes in people's faces from youth to age, probably discern the thing well enough, and feel a movement of pathos at their hearts in considering the world of trouble and emotion that is the causer of the changes. *That* old man's face was once like that little boy's! *That* little boy's will be one day like that old man's! What a thought to make us all love and respect one another, if not for our fine qualities, yet at least for the trouble and sorrow which we all go through!

Ay, and joy too; for all people have their joys as well as troubles, at one time or another, — most likely both together, or in constant alternation: and the greater part of troubles are not the worst things in the world, but only graver forms of the requisite motion of the universe, or workings towards a better condition of things, the greater or less violent according as we give them violence for violence, or respect them like awful but not ill-meaning gods, and entertain them with a rewarded patience. Grave thoughts, you will say, for Christmas. But no season has a greater right to grave thoughts, in passing; and, for that very reason, no season has a greater right to let them pass, and recur to more light ones.

So a noble and merry season to you, my masters; and may we meet, thick and threefold, many a time and oft, in blithe yet most thoughtful pages! Fail not to call to mind, in the course of the 25th of this month, that the divinest Heart that ever walked the earth was born on that day: and then smile and enjoy yourselves for the rest of it; for mirth is also of Heaven's making, and wondrous was the wine-drinking at Galilee.

THE END.

Boston: Printed by John Wilson and Son.

www.ingramcontent.com/pod-product-compliance
Lightning Source LLC
LaVergne TN
LVHW010217110826
845151LV00004B/1118

* 9 7 8 1 4 2 5 5 2 7 9 2 1 *